Creative Mathematics

Part I Book 8

Suitable for Students of Grade VIII of

National and State Boards

Chandan Sukumar Sengupta

Basics of Mathematics Series

Creative Mathematics Part I Book 8

Suitable for Students of Grade VIII of National and State Boards.

First Publication: March, 2023

This workbook is prepared to equip students of grade 7th and 8th of National Curriculum having affinity to prosper in the field of Mathematics. It will also provide additional study materials with which students can enhance their mathematical skills. Most of the mathematical problems are incorporated in this book without any suggested solutions so as to make it usable and reusable during various instances of self-propelled study.

This Workbook is developed for the third time to meet the increasing demand of parents from various portions of the India and also from the other countries. This workbook will provide an ample scope of competency enhancement to students of Grade 7th and 8th and above. They will move on through different mathematical and daily life problems to bring back some refinements in their basic understanding. The task of updating and reproducing the reference contents is also made with an objective of providing some background study materials to students having urgency to move on through self-propelled practices. Some experiences of previous class will be handled to link up the horizontal correlations of principal areas of competencies.

One can use this workbook for gaining adequate confidence related to IMO and other allied examinations which are periodically conducted by different boards of studies. Newly added aid boxes are useful for accelerating the pace of learning and also for providing additional scope of moving through exercise of memory and intellect. It will also provide keyterms and definitions related to mathematics and data science.

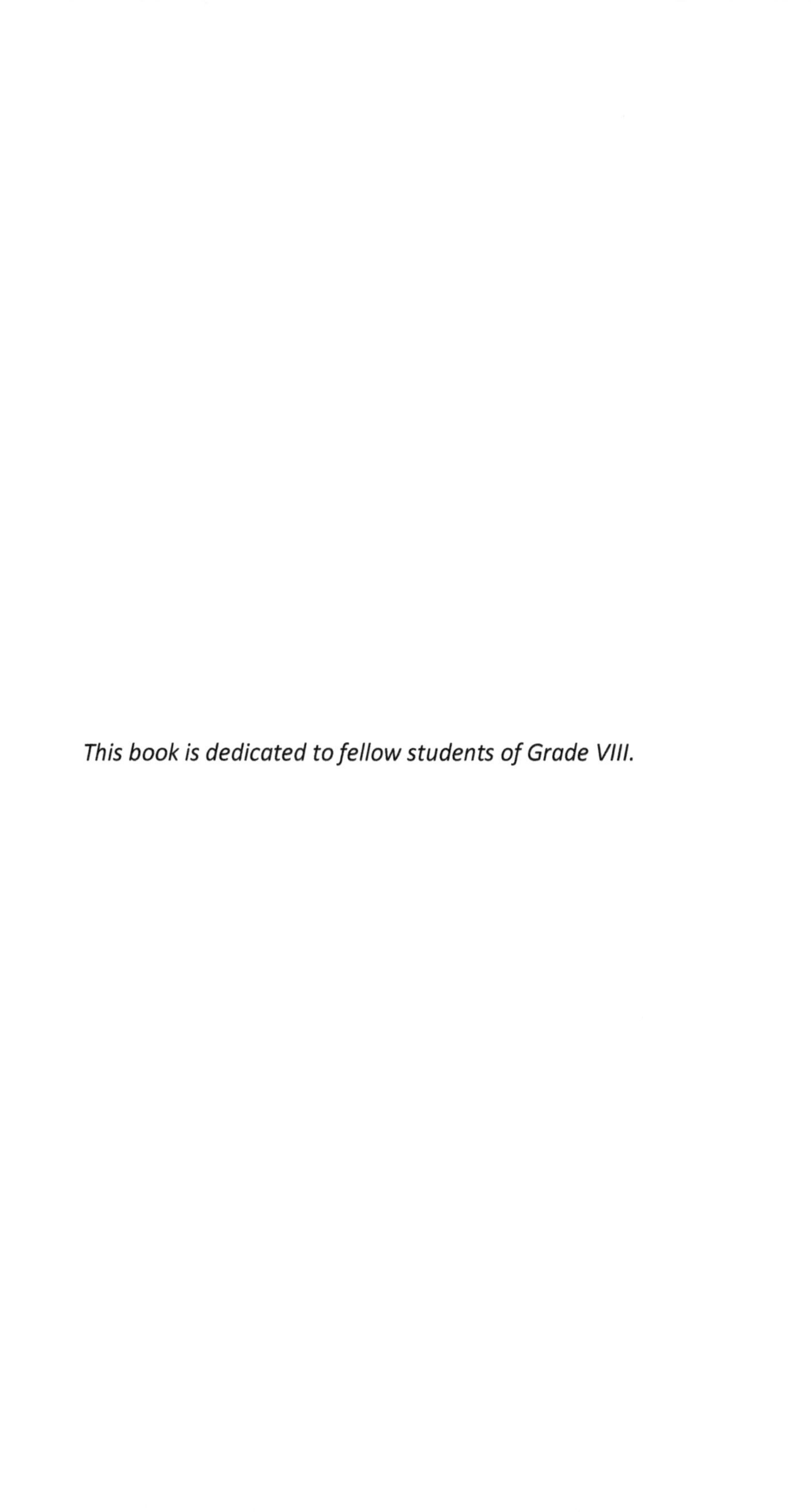

This book is dedicated to fellow students of Grade VIII.

Contents

CONTENTS

Revision

Before moving on it would be better if we recollect all our understanding related to the terms and definitions related to Mathematics.

Definitions

A

1. **Absolute value**
Distance of a number from 0. It is always a positive number.

2. **Abundant numbers**
Number less than the sum of its proper divisors.

3. **Acute angle**
Angle less than 90 radians. Lies between 0° and 90°.

4. **Acute triangle**
Triangle having three acute angles.

5. **Addend**
A number added to another number.

6. **Addition**
Process of taking sum of two or more numbers.

7. **Addition Property of Equality**
The sides remain equal if we add or subtract same number on both sides of equation.

8. **Additive inverse**
A number added to another number to get zero.

9. **Adjacent angles**
Angles that do not overlap having common side and common vertex.

10. **Algebra**
Branch of mathematics deals with mathematics symbols.

11. **Algebraic equation**
An equation attained by equating to zero a sum of a finite number of terms each one of which is a product of positive integral powers.

12. **Algebraic expression**
A specific arrangement of variables, algebraic operators, and integer constants.

13. Algebraic numbers
A complex number that is a root of a non-zero polynomial in one variable with rational coefficients.
14. Alphametic numbers
A mathematical puzzle where each letter stands for a digit from 0 to 9.
15. Amicable numbers
Two different numbers associated in such a way that the addition of the proper divisors of each is equal to the other number.
16. Angle
A figure formed by two lines having a common endpoint.
17. Angle measure
Measure of the angle formed by the two arms or rays at a mutual vertex.
18. Arc
A portion of the circumference of a circle.
19. Area
Quantity that indicates the extent of a two-dimensional shape in the plane.
20. Area of a circle
Measurement of a circle. $A = \pi r^2$
21. Area of a polygon
Amount of region or space occupied by a polygon.
22. Arithmetic
Branch of mathematics involves the study of numbers and traditional operators.
23. Arithmetic expression
An expression that uses addition, subtraction, multiplication, division, and exponentiation.
24. Arithmetic mean
Sum of all numerical values divided by total number of terms.
25. Arithmetic operations
Operations containing addition, subtraction, multiplication, and division.
26. Arrangement numbers
Number of ways that a number of things can be arranged or ordered.
27. Associative Law of Multiplication
Multiplying three or more numbers will not affect the result if grouping is altered.

28. **Associative Property**
Rearrangement of the parentheses in an expression will not change
the output.
29. **Automorphic numbers**
A natural number in a given number base whose square ends in the
same digits as the number itself.
30. **Average**
Sum of the numbers divided by how many numbers are being
averaged.
B
1. **Bar chart**
Presents categorical data with rectangular bars with lengths or
heights proportional to the values that they represent.
2. **Bar notation**
Method of writing digits repeating decimals using **bar** sign.
3. **Base**
Number of letters and combination of digits that a system of
counting uses to symbolize numbers.
4. **Base 10 system**
Decimal number system having 10 digits from 0 to 9.
5. **Bayes' Theorem**
A mathematical formula for determining conditional probability
named after British mathematician Thomas Bayes.
6. **Bell curve**
A type of continuous probability distribution for a real-valued
random variable.
7. **Biased sample**
The process used to generate the sample results in samples that are
methodically dissimilar from the population.
8. **Biconditional statement**
An arrangement of a conditional statement and its opposite written
in *if* and *only if* form.
9. **Bimodal**
Relating two modes, specifically of a statistical distribution having
two maxima.
10. **Binary numbers**
Numbers expressed in base-2 system involving only 2 digits 0 and 1.
11. **Binomial**
An algebraic expression of the sum or the difference of two terms.
12. **Binomial theorem**

Algebraic expansion of powers of a binomial.

13. Bisect

Dividing a line or segment in two parts.

14. Box-and-whisker graph

A process for graphically representing groups of numerical data through their quartiles.

15. Brackets

Symbols used for grouping expressions or equations.

C

1. Cardinal numbers

A broad view of the natural numbers used to measure the cardinality of sets.

2. Catalan numbers

Numbers that arrange a sequence of natural numbers that exist in several counting problems, frequently
containing recursively defined objects.

3. Center of a circle

Point that is at the equal distance from the edges of a circle.

4. Certain event

An event that is sure to happen.

5. Choice numbers

Number of ways that a number of things can be grouped or chosen.

6. Chord

A straight line segment whose endpoints both lie on the circle.

7. Circle

A round shaped figure that has no edges or corners.

8. Circular primes

A prime number with property that the number produced at every intermediate step when cyclically permuting its digits will be prime.

9. Circumference

Distance around the outside of the circle.

10. Closed figure

A figure whose start and end points are same.

11. Clustering

Depicting a group of data points, numbers or people that are located close together.

12. Combination

A method that defines the number of possible arrangements in a set of items where the order of the selection does not matter.

13. Commission

An amount paid for a service.

14. Commutative Property

Altering the order of the operands does not change the result.

15. Compatible numbers

Numbers that are easy to add, subtract, multiply, or divide mentally.

16. Complement of a set

A set having all elements in universal set except the elements of the set under complement.

17. Complementary angles

Two angles having sum of 90 degrees.

18. Complex fractions

A fraction in which the numerator and denominator or both have fractions.

19. Complex numbers

A **number** that can be expressed in the form a + bi.

20. Composite numbers

A positive integer that can be formed by multiplying two smaller positive integers.

21. Compound event

An **event** that has more than one possible results.

22. Compound interest

Interest on interest.

23. Compound statement

A sentence that contains two or more statements separated by logical connectors.

24. Conditional probability

Probability of one event happening with some relationship to one or more other events.

25. Conditional statement

A **statement** that can be written in the form "If *A* then *B*.

26. Cone

A three-dimensional geometric shape having flat base.

27. Congruent figures

Figures identical in shape.

28. Congruent numbers

A positive integer that is the area of a right triangle with three rational number sides.

29. Congruent polygons

Polygons of same size and shape.

30. Constant
A value that doesn't change.

31. Convenience sample
Involves the sample being drawn from that part of the population that is close to hand.

32. Coordinate
A system that uses one or more numbers, or coordinates, to uniquely determine the position of the points.

33. Coordinate plane
A Cartesian coordinate system that specifies each point on a plane.

34. Corresponding angles
Angles formed when two parallel lines are crossed by a line.

35. Cross products
A vector c that is perpendicular to both a and b, with a direction given by the right-hand rule and a magnitude equal to the area of the parallelogram that the vectors span.

36. Cube
A three-dimensional solid object bounded by six square faces or sides with all three meeting at each vertex.

37. Cubic numbers
A number multiplied to itself three times.

38. Cumulative frequency
Total frequency in a frequency distribution.

39. Customary measurement system
A set of measures and weights used for measuring temperature, capacity, length, and weight.

40. Cyclic numbers
An integer in which cyclic permutations of the digits are succeeding integer multiples of the number.

41. Cylinder
A three-dimensional surface with the surface shaped by the points at a fixed distance from a given line segment, known as the axis.

D

1. Data
Collection of words, measurements, numbers, etc.

2. Data set
A collection or grouping of words, measurements, numbers or observations.

3. Decimal
A dots that specifies the values in tenths, hundredths, etc.

4. Decimal digits
Digits from 0 to 9.
5. Decimal fraction
A fraction where the denominator is a power of ten.
6. Decimal numbers
Numbers from 0 to 9, having base-10.
7. Decimal point
A dot or point used to separate the whole number part from the fractional part of a number.
8. Decimal system
System that uses a notation in which each number is expressed in base 10 by using numbers from 0 to 9.
9. Deficient number
A **number** *n* for which the sum of divisors of "*n*" is less than *2n.*
10. Degree
The largest exponent the variable has in a polynomial with one variable.
11. Degrees
A measurement of a plane angle in which one full rotation is 360 degrees.
12. Denominator
A number occurs below the line in a fraction.
13. Dependent events
Two events are dependent if the result of the first affects the result of the second so that the probability is altered.
14. Diameter
A line passed through the center of circle whose endpoints touches the circle.
15. Difference
Result of subtracting one number from another.
16. Digital root
Value acquired by an iterative procedure of summing digits, on each iteration using the outcome from the former iteration to compute a digit sum.
17. Dimension
Minimum number of coordinates needed to specify any point within it.
18. Discount
A deduction from the usual cost of something.
19. Disjoint

Having no common elements in two sets.

20. Disjunction

A compound statement formed by joining two statements with the connector OR.

21. Distributive Property of Multiplication

Multiplying two numbers will result in the same thing as breaking up one factor into two addends, multiplying both addends by the other factor, and adding together both products.

22. Dividend

A number being divided.

23. Divisibility rule

A way of defining whether a given integer is **divisible** by a fixed divisor without performing the division.

24. Division

A process of distribution of numbers or objects.

25. Division Property of Equality

When we divide both sides of an equation by the same non-zero number, the two sides remain equal.

26. Divisor

A number used to divide the dividend.

E

1. Edge

A type of line joining two sides or vertices.

2. Egyptian fractions

Sum of finitely many rational numbers, each of which can be written in the form q1, where q is a positive integer.

3. Ellipsis

Set of all points on a plane whose distance from two fixed points F and G add up to a constant.

4. Empty set

A set having no element.

5. Equality

State of being equal or having same value.

6. Equation

A statement that asserts the equality of two expressions, which are linked by the equals sign "=".

7. Equilateral triangle

A triangle in which all three sides have the same length.

8. Equivalent

Two quantities or values being same.

9. Equivalent decimals

Decimals having same value.

10. Equivalent fractions

Fractions having same value but numerator and denominator are different.

11. Equivalent ratios

Ratios having same value.

12. Even numbers

Numbers that can be competent divided by 2.

13. Expanded form

A way of writing numbers to see the math value of individual digits.

14. Experiment

An approach to investigate objects and its properties.

15. Experimental probability

Probability determined on the basis of the results of an experiment repeated many times.

16. Exponent

The number of times a number is multiplied by itself.

17. Expression

A finite combination of signs and symbols that is well-formed according to rules that depend on the context.

F

1. Factor numbers

Numbers multiply to get another number.

2. Factor tree

A diagram used to determine the prime factors of a natural number greater than one.

3. Factorial numbers

The product of all the integers from 1 to that number.

4. Fibonacci Numbers

Each number is the sum of the two preceding ones, starting from 0 and 1.

5. Fibonacci Sequence

Each number is the sum of the two preceding ones, starting from 0 and 1.

6. Figurate numbers

A number that can be represented by a regular geometrical arrangement of equally spaced points.

7. Finite

Limited to an extent.

8. Finite set
A set that has a limited number of elements.
9. Fractal
A class of complex geometric shapes that commonly have fractional dimension.
10. Fraction
A number that represents a part of a whole.
11. Fraction bar
A visual illustration of fractions which aids in
comparing fractions and carrying out operations with fractions.
12. Frequency table
A table that lists items and expresses the number of times the items occur.
13. Function
A binary relation between two sets that links every component of the first set to exactly one element of the second set.
14. Fundamental Counting Principle
If there are s ways to do one thing, and r ways to do another thing, then there are s×r ways to do both things.

G
1. Geometry
Branch of mathematics that studies the shapes, angles, positions, sizes, and dimensions of things.
2. Gnomon
A rectangle with another rectangle cut out of one corner.
3. Goldbach's Conjecture
Every even whole number greater than 2 is the sum of two prime numbers.
4. Golden Ratio
Two quantities are in the golden ratio if their ratio is the equivalent as the ratio of their sum to the larger of the two quantities (1.618).
5. Golden Rectangle
A rectangle whose side lengths are in the golden ratio.
6. Graph
Visual representation of quantities or expressions on a plane.
7. Greater than
Relationship between two quantities depicting one is greater than other.
8. Greatest
Largest number in a set.

9. Greatest common factor (GCF)
Highest number that divides exactly into two or more numbers.
10. Grid
Coordinate plane containing a space of small squares, with an x-axis and y-axis.
11. Grid lines
Lines that cross the chart plot to show axis divisions.
12. Gyrating numbers
Numbers whose digits increase and decrease in a continuous repetitive cycle.

H
1. Happy numbers
A number which eventually reaches 1 when replaced by the sum of the square of each digit.
2. Harshad number
An integer that is divisible by the sum of its digits when written in the given base.
3. Height
Measurement from base to top.
4. Helix
A smooth space curve with tangent lines at a constant angle to a fixed axis (i.e., spiral staircase).
5. Hexagon
A six-sided polygon or 6-gon. Angles totaling to 720 degree.
6. Histogram
 A graphical display of data using bars of different heights.
7. Horizontal bar
A line used to indicate that the expression is to be considered grouped together.
8. Horizontal scale
Multiplies or dividing every x-coordinate by a constant while leaving the y-coordinate unchanged.
9. Hypotenuse
Lengthiest side of a right-angled triangle, the side opposite the right angle.
10. Hypothesis
A proposed explanation for a phenomenon.

I
1. Identity Property of One
Any number multiplied by **1** stays the same.

2. Identity Property of Zero
Any number added or subtracted to zero stays the same.

3. Imaginary number
Square root of a negative number that does not have a tangible value, multiplied by the imaginary unit i.

4. Impossible event
An event that cannot happen.

5. Improper fraction
A fraction in which the numerator is greater than or equal to the denominator.

6. Independent events
An event that has no link to another event's chances of occurring or not occurring.

7. Indirect measurement
A process of using proportions to find an unidentified length or distance in same figures.

8. Inequality
Having terms or numbers not equal.

9. Infinite number
A number that is not limited to an extent.

10. Infinite set
A set having unlimited number of objects or numbers.

11. Integer operations
Operations performed on integers such as addition, subtraction, etc.

12. Integers
A number that can be written without a fractional component.

13. Intersecting lines
Lines crossing or bisecting each other at some point.

14. Intersection
Act of crossing a line.

15. Interval
A set of real numbers that comprises of all real numbers lying between any two numbers of the set.

16. Inverse operations
An operation that undoes what was done by the previous operation.

17. Irrational number
A real number that cannot be written as a simple fraction.

18. Isosceles triangle
A triangle having two sides of the same length.

J
1. Jefferson Method
A type of party-list proportional representation, highest averages method for allotting seats.

K
1. Keith Number
A natural number in a number base with digits such that when a sequence is created, such that the first terms are the digits of and each subsequent term is the sum of the previous terms, is part of the sequence.
2. Knot
A closed non-self-intersecting curve that is implanted in three dimensions and cannot be untied to make a simple loop.

L
1. Lateral faces
The faces in a prism or pyramid that are not bases.
2. Leading zero
Any 0 digit that comes before the first nonzero digit in a number string in positional notation.
3. Least common denominator (LCD)
Smallest number that can be a common denominator for a set of fractions.
4. Least common multiple (LCM)
 Smallest positive number that is a multiple of two or more numbers.
5. Leg
A leg of geometrical shape is one of its sides.
6. Length
Any arbitrarily chosen and accepted reference standard for measurement.
7. Less than
Relationship between two numbers depicting inequality.
8. Like terms
Terms that have the same powers and variables.
9. Line
A one- dimensional straight figure that has no thickness and extends infinitely in both directions.
10. Line chart
A chart formed by joining the points given by the data with straight lines.

11. Line graph
A graph formed by linking the points given by the data with straight lines.

12. Line of symmetry
The axis or imaginary line that passes through the center of the object or shape and divides it into equal halves.

13. Line plot
Type of plot which shows information as a series of data points known as markers joined by straight line segments.

14. Line segment
A line that is confined by two separate end points, and holds every point on the line between its endpoints.

15. Logical connector
Combines simple statements into compound statements.

16. Logically equivalent
If two statements or expressions have same truth values for each possible substitution for their variables.

17. Long division
A standard division algorithm appropriate for dividing multi-digit numbers that is simple enough to perform by hand.

18. Lower extreme
The least value in the data set.

19. Lower quartile
Middle number that occurs between the least value of the dataset and the median.

20. Lowest terms
The form of a fraction in which the numerator and denominator have no factor in common except 1.

M

1. Map scale
The ratio of a distance on the map to the corresponding distance on the ground.

2. Mean
Sum of the values divided by the number of values.

3. Measure of central tendency
A single value that attempts to determine a set of data by recognizing the central position within that set of data.

4. Median
A value splitting the greater half from the lower half of a data sample or a population.

5. **Mental arithmetic**
Arithmetical calculations using only the human brain, with no help from any devices.
6. **Mersenne numbers**
A prime number that is one less than a power of two.
7. **Metric system**
A system of measurement that uses the liter, meter and gram as base **units** of capacity, weight, and length.
8. **Midpoint**
Middle point of a line which is equal from endpoints.
9. **Mixed number**
A whole number and a proper fraction represented together.
10. **Mode**
Value that appears most often in a set of data values.
11. **Monodigit numbers**
A natural number composed of repeated instances of the same digit.
12. **Multiple**
An outcome after multiplying the number by an integer.
13. **Multiple-bar graph**
A graph used to show relationship between different values of data using bars.
14. **Multiple-line graph**
A graph used to display relationship between different values of data using lines.
15. **Multiples**
A number that can be divided by another number a certain number of times without a remainder.
16. **Multiplication**
Operation of obtaining product of two numbers.
17. **Multiplication Property of Equality**
Having same equality after multiplying both sides of an equation by same number.
18. **Multiply perfect number**
A number N is said to be Multiply-perfect numbers if N divides sigma (N), where sigma (N) = sum of all divisors of N.
19. **Mutually exclusive**
A statistical term illustrating two or more events that cannot happen at the same time.
N

1. **Narcissistic numbers**
Numbers that can be expressed by some kind of mathematical manipulation of their digits.
2. **Natural numbers**
Numbers used for counting and ordering 1, 2, 3, 4, 5,...., .
3. **Negation**
An operation that takes a proposition to another proposition "not ", written, or.
4. **Negative integer**
A whole number that has value less than zero.
5. **Null set**
Set having no value at all.
6. **Number line**
A straight line with numbers positioned at equal segments or intervals along its length.
7. **Number sequences**
A list of numbers that are linked by a rule.
8. **Number theory**
A study of properties of the integers.
9. **Numerator**
A number above the line in a vulgar fraction.
10. **Numerical expression**
A mathematical sentence involving only numbers and one or more operation signs.

O

1. **Object**
Anything that has been formally defined.
2. **Oblong numbers**
A number which is the product of two consecutive integers, that is, a number of the form n.
3. **Obtuse angle**
Angle greater than 90° but less than 180°.
4. **Obtuse triangle**
Triangle having one obtuse angle.
5. **Octagon**
An eight-sided polygon or 8-gon.
6. **Octahedral numbers**
A figurate number that shows the number of spheres in an octahedron shaped from close-packed spheres.
7. **Odd Numbers**

A number that leaves a remainder when divided by 2.

8. Opposites

Inverse of each other.

9. Order of operations

A collection of procedures that reflect conventions about which procedures to perform first in order to calculate a given mathematical expression.

10. Ordered pair

A pair of numbers of variables in which the order of the objects is important and is used to differentiate and identify the pair.

11. Ordering fractions

Arranging fraction either from the smallest to the largest or largest to smallest.

12. Ordinal numbers

Number that describes the position of something in a list.

13. Origin

A special point used as a fixed point of reference for the geometry of the surrounding space.

14. Outcome

The result of a calculation in an undergoing evaluation.

15. Outlier

A data point that varies considerably from other observations.

16. Overestimate

An estimate that is too high surpassing the actual outcome.

17. Overlapping sets

Two sets having at least one element in common.

P

1. Palindrome number

A number that remains the unchanged when its digits are reversed.

2. Pandigital number

A pandigital number is an integer that in a given base has among its significant digits each digit used in the base at least once.

3. Parallel lines

Two lines in a plane that do not intersect each other.

4. Parallelogram

A quadrilateral with two pairs of parallel sides.

5. Parasite numbers

Numbers that keeps the exact same digits when divided or multiplied by another number.

6. Parentheses

Brackets used to specify order of evaluation.

7. Partial products

Multiplying each digit of a number in turn with each digit of another where each digit keeps its position.

8. Pascal's Triangle

A triangular array created by summing adjacent elements in preceding rows.

9. Pentagon

Five-sided polygon having sum of internal angles of 540 degree.

10. Pentatope numbers

A number in the fifth cell of any row of Pascal's triangle starting with the 5-term row 1 4 6 4 1 either from left to right or from right to left.

11. Percent

A ratio or number that represents a fraction of 100.

12. Percent change

Change in a percentage from start to end.

13. Percent decrease

A measure of percent change which is the extent to which something drops value.

14. Percent increase

A measure of percent change which is the extent to which something gains value.

15. Percent symbol

Symbol used to indicate a percentage **"%"**.

16. Percentage

A number or ratio expressed as a fraction of 100.

17. Perfect numbers

A positive integer that is equal to the sum of its positive divisors, except the number itself.

18. Perimeter

Distance around a two-dimensional space.

19. Period

Length from one peak to next in a periodic function.

20. Periodic numbers

Numbers that can be expressed as an integral of an algebraic function over an algebraic domain.

21. Permutable prime

A number that remains prime on every reordering of the digits.

22. Perpendicular lines

Two lines that meet or intersect each other at right angles 90°.

23. **Persistent numbers**

The sequential product of whose digits, ultimately produces a single digit number.

24. **Pi**

Mathematical constant with a value of *3.14159.*

25. **Pi Day**

Annual celebration of the constant Pi celebrated on March 14 every year.

26. **Pie chart**

A circular statistical graphic, which is divided into portions to demonstrate numerical proportion.

27. **Place value**

Value of each digit in a number.

28. **Plane**

A two-dimensional flat surface that spreads infinitely far.

29. **Plane figure**

A geometric figure that has no thickness and lies completely in one plane.

30. **Point**

Element of space with no width, length or size.

31. **Point of rotation**

A central point around which a figure is rotated.

32. **Polygon**

Closed curve involving a set of line segments linked in a way that no two segments cross.

33. **Polygonal numbers**

A number represented as pebbles or dots organized in the shape of a regular polygon.

34. **Polyhedron**

A three-dimensional shape with sharp corners or vertices, straight edges, and flat polygonal faces.

35. **Positive**

Number greater than zero.

36. **Positive integers**

Natural numbers used for counting 1, 2, 3, 4…,.

37. **Power**

Demonstrates how many times to use the number in a multiplication.

38. **Precision**

Number of digits used to perform a given computation.

39. Prime factorization

Breaking a number down into the set of **prime** numbers which multiply together to outcome in the original number.

40. Prime number

Number that is divisible only by itself and 1.

41. Principal

The total amount of money loaned out or invested, not involving any dividends or interest.

42. Prism

A polyhedron comprising an n-sided polygonal base, a second base which is a translated copy of the first, and n other faces joining corresponding sides of the two bases.

43. Probability

Branch of mathematics regarding numerical descriptions of how likely an event is to happen, or how likely it is that a proposition is correct.

44. Probability theory

Branch of mathematics concerned with probability.

45. Product

Process of multiplying two or more numbers.

46. Product perfect numbers

Product of all divisors of the number, other than itself, is equal to the number.

47. Pronic numbers

A number which is the product of two consecutive integers, that is, a number of the form $n(n + 1)$.

48. Proper fraction

A fraction where the numerator is less than the denominator.

49. Proper subset

Subset of A that is not equal to A.

50. Proportion

A number in comparative relationship with a whole.

51. Protractor

A measuring instruments for measuring angles.

52. Pyramid

A polyhedron formed by connecting a polygonal base and a point, called the apex.

53. Pyramidal numbers

A figurate number that represents a pyramid with a polygonal base and a given number of triangular sides.

54. Pythagorean Theorem

Area of the square with hypotenuse side is equal to the sum of the areas of the squares on the other two sides.

Q

1. Quadrants

The axes of a two-dimensional Cartesian system divide the plane into four infinite regions.

2. Quadratic equations

Equation that can be reordered in standard form as
where x represents an unknown, and a, b, and c represent known numbers.

3. Quadratic formula

Formula that provides the solution to a quadratic equation.

4. Quadrilateral

A two-dimensional closed shape which has four straight sides.

5. Quasi perfect numbers

A natural number n for which the sum of all its divisors is equal to $2n + 1$.

6. Quotient

A number or quantity produced by the division of two numbers.

R

1. Radius

A straight line from the center to the circumference of a sphere or circle.

2. Radii

Plural of radius.

3. Random number

A number selected as if by chance from some specified distribution such that selection of a large set of these numbers regenerates the underlying distribution.

4. Random sample

A sample that is chosen randomly from a larger data set.

5. Range

Difference between the greatest and lowest values.

6. Rate

Ratio between two related quantities in different units.

7. Ratio
The quantifiable relation between two numbers or quantities expressing the number of times one value includes or is contained within the other.

8. Rational number
A number that can be expressed as fraction or quotient of two integers.

9. Ray
A part of line that has fixed starting point but no ending point.

10. Real numbers
Number that can have both rational and irrational numbers.

11. Reasonable estimate
An estimate that does not exceeds the original answer of the calculation.

12. Reciprocal
Multiplicative inverse of a number.

13. Rectangle
A quadrilateral having parallel sides equal to each other and four right angles.

14. Rectangular numbers
Numbers that can be arranged to shape a rectangle.

15. Rectangular prism
A 3-dimensional solid object having six faces that are rectangles.

16. Regular hexagon
A hexagon that is both equilateral and equiangular.

17. Regular pentagon
Pentagon having five sides whose interior angles are 108 degree.

18. Regular polygon
A polygon having all angles equal in measure and all sides of same length.

19. Relatively prime numbers
If there is no integer greater than 1 that divides two numbers, then they are relatively prime numbers.

20. Remainder
Number of amount left after a division.

21. Repeating decimal
Decimal illustration of a number whose digits are repeating its values at regular intervals and the infinitely repeated portion is not zero.

22. Repunit numbers

Number that includes repeated number of digit 1 and only included 1.

23. **Rhombus**

A quadrilateral whose four sides all have the same length.

24. **Right angle**

Angle of 90°.

25. **Right triangle**

Triangle having one right angle.

26. **Roman Numerals**

A number system developed in ancient Rome where letters such as X, I, V, L represent numbers.

27. **Roster notation**

A simple mathematical illustration of a set in mathematical form.

28. **Rotation (turn)**

A transformation in geometry in which an object is rotated about a fixed point called a point of rotation.

29. **Rotational symmetry**

Property of a shape which make it looks the same after some rotation by a partial turn.

30. **Round**

Shaped like a circle or cylinder.

S

1. **Sale price**

Price that has been set after adding some profit to the cost.

2. **Sales tax**

A tax paid to government for selling product or services to people.

3. **Sample**

A set of objects chosen or collected from a statistical population by a defined procedure.

4. **Sample space**

A set of possible outcomes of a random experiment.

5. **Scale**

Represents the relationship between measurement on the actual object and a measurement on a model.

6. **Scale drawing**

A drawing which has been enlarged or reduced from its original size, to a specified scale.

7. **Scalene triangle**

A triangle in which all three sides have dissimilar lengths and all three angles have different measures.

8. Scatterplot

A type of data representation that displays the relationship between two numerical variables.

9. Scientific notation

A way of writing very large or very small numbers.

10. Sectors

Portion of a disk surrounded by an arc and two radii, where the larger being the major sector and the smaller area is known as the minor sector.

11. Self-similarity

Object approximately or exactly similar to a part of itself.

12. Semiperfect numbers

A natural number that is equal to the sum of all or some of its proper divisors.

13. Sequence

A sequence is a counted collection of objects in which recurrences are permissible and order matters.

14. Set

A collection of objects or elements.

15. Set equality

Elements or members of two sets are same.

16. Set notation

Used for describing a set by numbering its elements, or declaring the properties that its members must fulfil.

17. Set theory

Branch of mathematical logic that studies sets, which informally are collections of objects.

18. Set-builder notation

Mathematical notation for determining a set by numbering its elements, or declaring the properties that its members must fulfil.

19. Sieve of Eratosthenes

Algorithm to find any prime numbers to a given extent.

20. Similar figures

Figures having congruent corresponding angles and equal side length.

21. Simulation

A method to model random events, so that simulated results closely match real-world results.

22. Sociable numbers

Numbers whose exact divisor sums form a cyclic sequence that starts and ends with the same number.

23. **Solid figure**
Three-dimensional objects having height, width, and length.

24. **Square**
A regular quadrilateral having four equal angles and four equal sides.

25. **Square numbers**
Number produced by multiplying to itself.

26. **Square root**
A value when multiplied to itself gives the original number.

27. **Squarefull number**
A number that has at least a square in its prime factorization.

28. **Standard form**
Method of representing numbers that are too small or too large.

29. **Stem-and-leaf plot**
Table for displaying measureable data in a graphical format, like a histogram, to assist in visualizing the shape of a distribution.

30. **Straight angle**
An angle equal to 180 degree.

31. **Straight commission**
Commission only earned by making sales.

32. **Subset**
A set is subset of other set of it has all elements of that set.

33. **Subtraction**
Arithmetic operation that characterizes the operation of eliminating objects from a collection.

34. **Subtraction Property of Equality**
Equation will be the same if a number is subtracted from both sides of the equation.

35. **Sum**
Adding two or more numbers or variables.

36. **Superabundant numbers**
A natural number n where for all $m < n$ where σ denotes the sum-of-divisors function.

37. **Supplementary angles**
Angles whose sum is equal to 180 degree.

38. **Surface area**
A measure of the total area that the surface of the object occupies.

39. **Survey**

A list of questions intended at mining specific data from a specific group of people.

40. Symbolic Form

Sentence expressed in symbolic form uses logical connectors and symbols to represent the sentence logically.

41. Symbolic logic

Use of symbols to represent relations terms, and propositions in order to assist reasoning.

42. Systematic sample

Statistical approach having the selection of elements from an ordered sampling frame.

T

1. Table

Lists of numbers presenting the outcomes of a calculation with changing arguments.

2. Tag Numbers

Other names for numbers that are in our everyday use.

3. Tally table

Table with tally signs to represent a valuable data set.

4. Tautology

A statement or formula that is true in every possible explanation.

5. Taxicab numbers

The smallest integer that can be presented as a sum of two positive integer cubes in n distinct ways.

6. Terminating decimal

A decimal number that have finite number of digits after the decimal point.

7. Terms

Values on which the mathematical operations occur in an expression.

8. Tessellation

A pattern of shapes that fit perfectly together leaving no gaps on the surface.

9. Tetrahedral numbers

A figurate number that symbolizes a pyramid with three sides and a triangular base.

10. Theoretical probability

Probability that is determined on the basis of reasoning.

11. Three-dimensional

Object that can be measured in three dimensions such as height, width, and length.

12. Transcendental Numbers

A number that is not algebraic and not the root of a non-zero polynomial with rational coefficients.

13. Transformation

A function f that maps a set X to itself.

14. Translation (slide)

A motion in geometry in which an object is moved along a straight line without turning or changing the shape or size.

15. Trapezoid

A convex quadrilateral with at least one pair of parallel sides.

16. Trapezoidal numbers

A positive integer that can be expressed as the sum of two or more successive positive integers.

17. Tree diagram

Diagram used to represent a probability space.

18. Trend

A pattern in a set of results displayed in a graph.

19. Triangle

A polygon with three vertices and edges.

20. Triangular numbers

Numbers used to describe the pattern of dots that form larger and larger triangles.

21. Triple prime numbers

Three successive primes, such that the first and the last differ by six.

22. Truth table

Table that shows the truth-value of one or more compound propositions for every possible combination of truth-values of the propositions making up the compound ones.

23. Twin prime numbers

A prime number that is either 2 more or 2 less than another prime number.

U

1. Unbiased sample

A sample is an unbiased sample if every element or individual in the population has an equal chance of being chosen.

2. Underestimate

An estimate that is less than the original outcome to a calculation.

3. Union

Collection of all elements of two or more sets.

4. Unit fraction numbers

A rational number expressed as a **fraction** where the numerator is one and the denominator is a positive integer.

5. Unit rate

A rate with 1 in the denominator.

6. Universal set

A set which has elements of all the associated sets without any repetition of elements.

7. Unlike fractions

Fractions that don't have same denominators.

8. Upper extreme

Greatest value in the data set.

9. Upper quartile

Number dividing the 3rd and 4th quartile.

V

1. Variable

Symbol used to depict varying quantities or expressions.

2. Venn diagram

A drawing or demonstration that uses circles to represent the relationships among things or finite groups of things.

3. Vertex

A point or corner where lines meet.

4. Vertical angles

The angles opposite each other when two lines cross.

5. Vertical bar

A mathematical symbol used for various purposes such as to depict absolute value, determinant, or as an *OR* operator etc.

6. Vertical scale

Multiplies or divides each y-coordinate by a constant but leaving the x-coordinate unaffected.

7. Volume

Quantity of three-dimensional space surrounded by a closed surface.

W

1. Weight

Measure of how heavy an object is.

2. Whole numbers

A number that can be expressed without a fractional component.

3. Width

The measurement of the distance of a side of an object.

4. **Word form**

Method to write the numbers in descriptive form.

5. **Word problem**

Mathematical exercise where important contextual information on the problem is expressed in everyday language instead of mathematical notation.

X

1. **X-axis**

The line on a graph that runs from left to right (horizontally) through zero.

2. **X-coordinate**

X value in an **ordered pair** such as numbers paired together, are just two mathematical objects.

Y

1. **Y-axis**

The line on a graph that runs from top to bottom (vertically) through zero.

2. **Y-coordinate**

Y value in an **ordered pair** such as numbers paired together, are just two mathematical objects.

Z

1. **Zero**

A number in mathematics denoted by the symbol 0, used to show that no object is present.

Model Paper 1

A. Given a three digit number x + 5 + y where x is the digit at hundreds place and y is the digit at ones. If the number x + 5 + y is divisible by 9, find least positive value x + y ?

B. Product of two numbers is 18.75. If one number is three times the other, then find larger number.

C. The sum of the squares of the digits constituting a certain positive three-digit number is 74. The hundreds digit of the number is equal to the doubled sum of the digits in the tens and units places. Find the number if it is known that the difference between that number and the number written by the same digits in the reverse order is 495.

D. Show that exactly one of the numbers n, n + 2 or n + 4 is divisible by 3.

E. n(n + 1)(n + 5) is a multiple of 3.

F. The sum of the digits of a three-digit number is 11. If we subtract 594 from the number consisting of the same digits written in the reverse order, we shall get a required number. Find that three-digit number, if the sum of all pairwise products of the digits constituting that number is 31.

G. Pradeep gave away 8 sweets to his friends. This number was one-fifth of the number of sweets that he had with him at first. How many sweets did Pradeep have with him at first?

H. Some students planned a picnic. The budget for food was Rs. 480. But eight of these failed to go and thus the cost of food for each member increased by Rs. 10. How many students attended the picnic?

I: Sum total of sixth multiple of a natural number x and one fifth of the reciprocal of x is equal to 48.025. Find the value of $\sqrt[3]{x} + \sqrt[2]{x} + x + x^{-1} + x^{-2} + x^{-3}$

Model Paper 2

A.   A number is 27 more than the number obtained by reversing its digits. If its unit's and ten's digit are x and y respectively. write the linear equation representing the above statement.

B.   A three digit number 24 y is a multiple of 3, what might be the values of y?

C.   Find the least number which must be added to 6203 to obtain a perfect square. Also, find the square root of the number so obtained.

D.   Total number of 9 digit numbers that are divisible by 5, is equal to

E.   How many numbers greater than 40000 can be formed using the digits 1, 2, 3, 4 and 5 if each is used only once in a number?

F.   Find the number nearest to 110000 but greater than 100000 which is exactly divisible by each of 8,15 and 21.

G.   If the number of all 4-digit number whose product of digits is divisible by 3, are N,the

H.   Three normal AA_1, BB_1 and CC_1 are drawn from a point $P(h, k)$ to the parabola $y^2 = 4ax$, at A, B and C points. The following conditions are satisfied by the three normals.(i) any two of three normals are coincide(ii) $S(a, 0)$ be the focus of the parabola(iii) Three normals be real, then $h > 2a$(iv) Slopes of the normals are m_1, m_2 and m_3. If $m_1 m_2 = \lambda$, then the locus of P is a parabola(v) P lies on the line $y = \mu$, then the sides of the triangle ABC touch the parabola $S' = 0$.
SA SB SC is equal to.

I. Solve the following:

a) $9x^2 + 14x - 51 = 0$ b) $27x^3 - 64 = 0$ c) $81x^4 - 16 = 0$

d) one third of one sixteenth of $x^2 = 4,800$

e) $x^2 - x + 10 = (abc)^0$; Find the value of $x3 + 3x2 + 3x + 1$

f) Sum total of a number and its reciprocal is 25.04. Find the value of the square root of that number.

J. Solve the equation. Justify each step. Check your solution.

1. $x + 9 = 7$

2. $8.6 = z - 3.8$

3. $60 = -12r$

4. $\frac{3}{4}p = 18$

Solve the equation. Check your solution.

5. $2m - 3 = 13$

6. $5 = 10 - v$

7. $5 = 7w + 8w + 2$

8. $-21a + 28a - 6 = -10.2$

9. $2k - 3(2k - 3) = 45$

10. $68 = \frac{1}{5}(20x + 50) + 2$

Solve the equation.

11. $3c + 1 = c + 1$

12. $-8 - 5n = 64 + 3n$

13. $2(8q - 5) = 4q$

14. $9(y - 4) - 7y = 5(3y - 2)$

15. $4(g + 8) = 7 + 4g$

16. $-4(-5h - 4) = 2(10h + 8)$

17. To estimate how many miles you are from a thunderstorm, count the seconds between when you see lightning and when you hear thunder. Then divide by 5. Write and solve an equation to determine how many seconds you would count for a thunderstorm that is 2 miles away.

K. Solve the following:

1. Sum total of two digits of a two digit number is 9. After altering places of digits newly formed number is 9 more than the original number. Find sixth multiple of that number.
2. $9x2 + 41x - 78 = 0$. Find the value of x.

In Exercises 3–12, solve the literal equation for *y*.

3. $y - 3x = 13$
4. $2x + y = 7$

5. $2y - 18x = -26$
6. $20x + 5y = 15$

7. $9x - y = 45$
8. $6x - 3y = -6$

9. $4x - 5 = 7 + 4y$
10. $16x + 9 = 9y - 2x$

11. $2 + \frac{1}{6}y = 3x + 4$
12. $11 - \frac{1}{2}y = 3 + 6x$

In Exercises 13–22, solve the literal equation for *x*.
(See Example 2.)

13. $y = 4x + 8x$
14. $m = 10x - x$

15. $a = 2x + 6xz$
16. $y = 3bx - 7x$

17. $y = 4x + rx + 6$
18. $z = 8 + 6x - px$

19. $sx + tx = r$
20. $a = bx + cx + d$

21. $12 - 5x - 4kx = y$
22. $x - 9 + 2wx = y$

24. **MODELING WITH MATHEMATICS** The penny size of a nail indicates the length of the nail. The penny size *d* is given by the literal equation $d = 4n - 2$, where *n* is the length (in inches) of the nail.

   a. Solve the equation for *n*.

   b. Use the equation from part (a) to find the lengths of nails with the following penny sizes: 3, 6, and 10.

25. Two cisterns of identical rate of releasing water are used to refill four identical water tanks in 2 hours. Each of the cistern individually can refill individual water tank in ...... minutes.

L: Find the temperature in ^{0}C scale for which corresponding reading of ^{0}F will be two times greater.

M. $x^2 -22x + 120 = -1$; Find the value of $(x+1)^3 - (x-1)^3$

N. What fraction of all the numbers from 1 to 1000 are multiples of 250?

Model Paper 3

A. In the formula $p^4 - q^3 = r^2 - s$, make p as the subject of the formula.

(a) $p = (r^2 - q^3 - s)^{\frac{1}{4}}$

(b) $p = (r^2 - q^3 + s)^{\frac{1}{4}}$

(c) $p = (r^2 + q^3 + s)^{\frac{1}{4}}$

(d) $p = (r^2 + q^3 - s)^{\frac{1}{4}}$

B. The total surface area of a cuboid is $S = 2\,(lb + bh + lh)$. Make l as the subject of the formula.

(a) $l = \dfrac{S}{2(b + h)}$

(b) $l = \dfrac{S}{b + h} + \dfrac{bh}{b + h}$

(c) $l = \dfrac{S - 2bh}{2(b + h)}$

(d) $l = \dfrac{S - bh}{b + h}$

C. What are the auxiliary formulae of the statement "sum of the angles of a quadrilateral $ABCD$ is $360°$"

(If the four angles of the quadrilateral are A, B, C, and D)?

(a) $A = 360° - (B + C + D)$

H. In $P = \dfrac{5x + 2y}{3x - 4y}$, if $x = 5$ and $P = 7$, then $y =$ ________.

(a) 3

(b) $\dfrac{3}{8}$

(c) $\dfrac{8}{3}$

(d) $\dfrac{1}{3}$

I. In the formula $x = y + \sqrt{y^2 + 1}$, make y as the subject of the formula.

(a) $y = \dfrac{1}{2}(x^{-1} - x)$

(b) $y = \dfrac{1}{2}(x - x^{-1})$

(c) $y = \dfrac{1}{2}(x^{-1} + x)$

(d) $y = \dfrac{1}{2}\left(x^2 + \dfrac{1}{x}\right)$

J. In the formula $E = 3k\,(1 - 2c)$, make c as the subject of the formula.

(a) $c = \dfrac{1}{2} + \dfrac{E}{6k}$

(b) $c = \dfrac{1}{2} - \dfrac{E}{3k}$

(c) $c = \dfrac{1}{2} - \dfrac{E}{6k}$

(d) $c = \dfrac{1}{2} + \dfrac{E}{3k}$

K. If $\dfrac{1}{f} = \dfrac{1}{u} + \dfrac{1}{v}$, then make v as the subject of the formula.

D. If $S = \dfrac{a}{1 - r^3}$, then express r in terms of S and a.

(a) $r = \sqrt[3]{1 + \dfrac{a}{S}}$

(b) $r = \sqrt[3]{1 + \dfrac{S}{a}}$

(c) $r = \sqrt[3]{1 - \dfrac{S}{a}}$

(d) $r = \sqrt[3]{1 - \dfrac{a}{S}}$

In $S = ut + \dfrac{1}{2}at^2$, $S = 96$, $t = 8$, and $a = 2$. Find u.

(a) 2

(b) 8

(c) 4

(d) 1

E. If $C = \dfrac{5}{9}\,(F - 32)$, then express F in terms of C.

(a) $F = \dfrac{9}{5}\,C - 32$

(b) $F = 32 - \dfrac{9}{5}\,C$

(c) $F = \dfrac{9}{5}\,(C + 32)$

(d) $F = \dfrac{9}{5}\,C + 32$

F. If $a = b - \sqrt{b^2 - 1}$, then express b in terms of a.

(a) $b = \dfrac{1}{2}(a^{-1} - a)$

(b) $b = \dfrac{1}{2}(a + a^{-1})$

(c) $b = \dfrac{1}{2}(a - a^{-1})$

(d) $b = \dfrac{-1}{2}(a + a^{-1})$

G. If $\dfrac{1}{a} + \dfrac{1}{b} = \dfrac{1}{c} + \dfrac{1}{d}$, then express a in terms of b, c, and d.

(a) $a = \dfrac{bcd}{bc + cd - bd}$

(b) $a = \dfrac{bcd}{cd + bd - bc}$

L. The sum of a^2 and cb^3 equals the sum of twice to d and thrice to c. Express b in terms of a, c, and d.

(a) $b = \sqrt[3]{\dfrac{1}{c}\left(2d + 3c - a^2\right)}$

(b) $b = \dfrac{1}{c}\sqrt[3]{2d + 3c - a^2}$

(c) $b = \dfrac{\sqrt[3]{a^2} - 2d - 3c}{c}$

(d) $b = \sqrt[3]{\dfrac{1}{c}\left(2d + 3c + a^2\right)}$

M. In $c = \dfrac{22a + 9b}{3a + 2b}$, $c = 6$ and $a = 3$, find b.

(a) 6

(b) 2

(c) 4

(d) 8

The curved surface area (c) of a cone is $\pi r l$, where $l = \sqrt{r^2 + h^2}$, express h in terms of c and r.

(a) $h = \dfrac{1}{\pi r}\sqrt{c^2 - \pi^2 r^4}$

(b) $h = \dfrac{1}{\pi r}\sqrt{c - \pi^2 r^2}$

(c) $h = \dfrac{1}{\pi r}\sqrt{c^2 - \pi^2 r^2}$

(d) $h = \dfrac{1}{\pi r}\sqrt{c + \pi^2 r^4}$

1. Self Evaluation

All the worksheets are prepared on the basis of content areas of Mathematics Evaluation (CCE)

Worksheet 1

I: Identify the missing options

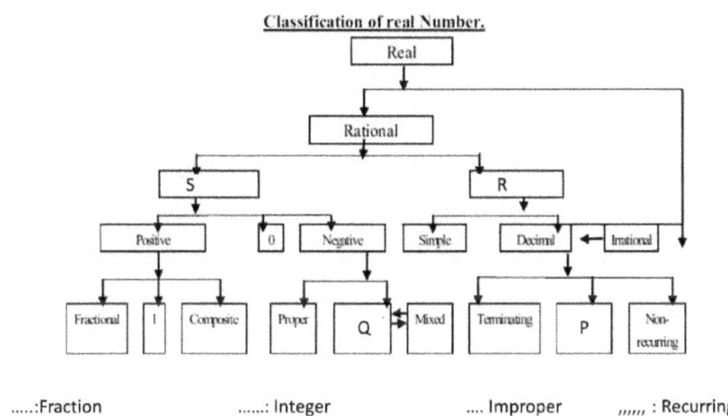

.....:Fraction   ......: Integer   .... Improper   ,,,,,, : Recurring

II: Options related property of rational numbers is as follows…

A: All rational numbers can be expressed in the form of p/q in which q is not equal to zero.

B: Rational numbers can be placed on a number line.

C: All integers can be expressed in the form of rational numbers, but all the rational numbers cannot be expressed in integer.

D: Rational numbers are represented by using two co-prime integers.

Find if any of the above mentioned option requires modification.

III: Statements related to terminating and non-terminating decimals are as follows:

Terminating decimals : In terminating decimals, the finite numbers of digits are in the right side of a decimal points. Ƀr example,   0.12,1.023,7.832,54.67,.......... etc. are terminating decimals.

Recurring decimals : In recurring decimals, the digits or the part of the digits in the right side of the decimal points will occar repeatedly. Ƀr example, 3.333....., 2.454545......, 5.12765765.......... etc. are recurring decimals.

Non-terminating decimals : In non-terminating decimals, the digits in the right side of a decimal point never terminate, i.e., the number of digits in the right side of decimal point will not be finite neither will the part occur repeatedly. Ƀr example.1.4142135......, 2.8284271....... etc. are non-terminating decimals.

Terminating decimals and recurring decimals are rational numbers and non-terminating decimals are irrational numbers. The value of an irrational number can be determined upto the required number after the decimal point. If the numerator and denominator of a fraction can be expressed in natural numbers, that fraction is a rational number.

Classify the decimals stating reasons:

a. 5.2333...   b. 0.0025   c. 0.105105 ......   d. 0.450123

d. $\sqrt{0.0625}$ e. 2.1356124 ....   f. $\sqrt[3]{0.001331}$ g. 0.121121

h. $\sqrt[4]{0.0256}$ i. 3.120304   j. $\sqrt[5]{0.03125}$ k. 121.0121

IV: Is cube root of -125 is a rational number?

V: Solve the following ...

Example   Express $42.34\dot{7}\dot{8}$ into simple fraction.

Solution : $42.34\dot{7}\dot{8}$ = 42.347878........

So, $42.34\dot{7}\dot{8} \times 10000$ = 42.347878.........× 10000 = 42348.7878

and $42.34\dot{7}\dot{8} \times 100$ = 42.347878........ × 100   = 4234.7878

Subtracting, $42.34\dot{7}\dot{8} \times 90$ = 423478 – 4234

Therefore, $42.34\dot{7}\dot{8} = \dfrac{423478 - 4234}{90} = \dfrac{41944}{90} = \dfrac{3497}{825} = 42\dfrac{287}{825}$

Required fraction is $42\dfrac{287}{825}$

On the basis of above example convert the following repeated decimal into simple fraction.

a. 31.1212....   b. 0.1010101,,,,,   c. 11.333........

d. 21.12353535...   e. 11.010101   f. 90.090909.....

g. 121.032032032....

VI. Observe the example and solve the questions as follows.

Add : $3 \cdot \overset{\cdot}{8}\overset{\cdot}{9}$, $2 \cdot 1\overset{\cdot}{7}\overset{\cdot}{8}$ and $5 \cdot 89\overset{\cdot}{7}9\overset{\cdot}{8}$

Solution : Here the number of digits in the non-recurring part will be 2 and the number of digits in the recurring part will be 6 which is L.C.M. of 2,2 and 3.

At first three recurring decimals are made similar.

$3 \cdot \overset{\cdot}{8}\overset{\cdot}{9}$ $= 3 \cdot \overset{\cdot}{8}9898989$

$2 \cdot 1\overset{\cdot}{7}\overset{\cdot}{8}$ $= 2 \cdot 1\overset{\cdot}{2}78787\overset{\cdot}{8}$

$5 \cdot 89\overset{\cdot}{7}9\overset{\cdot}{8}$ $= \underline{5 \cdot 89\overset{\cdot}{7}98798}$

                   $11 \cdot 97576574$

$[8 + 8 + 7 + 2 = 25$, Here 2 is the number to
be carried over, 2 of 25 has been added.$]$

             $\underline{+ 2}$

                 $11 \cdot 9757657\overset{\cdot}{6}$

The required sum is $11 \cdot 9\overset{\cdot}{7}57657\overset{\cdot}{6}$ or $11 \cdot 9\overset{\cdot}{7}57\overset{\cdot}{6}$

Remark : In the sum the number in the recurring part is 575675. But the value is not changed if 576 is taken as the number of recurring part.

Note : To make clear the concept of adding 2 at the extreme right side, this addition is done in another method :

Similarly add the following: ----

A: 3.333... + 4.444... + 5.5555... + 6.666... = ...

B: 11.1010..... + 12.1212..... + 13.1313..... = ...

C: 15.1212.... + 16.1616.... + 17.1717.... = ...

D: 101.101101.... + 103.103103 ..... + 104.104104..... = ...

VII: Arrange the following in ascending order.

A: 11.1111..., 10.9999...., 11.10101010..., 10.909090..., 9.090909....

B: 8.125, 8.125125...., 8.126, 8.110110.... , 8.9898....

C: 12.101101101 = ... [Write in the form of a simple fraction.]

VIII: Sum total of a natural number and Its reciprocal is equal to 8.125. Find the sum total of sixth and tenth multiple of that natural number.

IX: Middle number of five consecutive odd numbers is 121. Find the sum total of first and fifth number.

Worksheet 2

1. Find the square with the help of the formulae :

(a) $2a + 3b$ (b) $2ab + 3bc$ (c) $x^2 + \dfrac{2}{y^2}$ (d) $a + \dfrac{1}{a}$ (e) $4y - 5x$ (f) $ab - c$

(g) $5x^2 - y$ (h) $x + 2y + 4z$ (i) $3p + 4q - 5r$ (j) $3b - 5c - 2a$ (k) $ax - by - cz$

(l) $a - b + c - d$ (m) $2a + 3x - 2y - 5z$ (n) 101 (o) 997 (p) 1007

2. Simplify :

(a) $(2a + 7)^2 + 2(2a + 7)(2a - 7) + (2a - 7)^2$

(b) $(3x + 2y)^2 + 2(3x + 2y)(3x - 2y) + (3x - 2y)^2$

(c) $(7p + 3r - 5x)^2 - 2(7p + 3r - 5x)(8p - 4r - 5x) + (8p - 4r - 5x)^2$

(d) $(2m + 3n - p)^2 + (2m - 3n + p)^2 - 2(2m + 3n - p)(2m - 3n + p)$

(e) $6 \cdot 35 \times 6 \cdot 35 + 2 \times 6 \cdot 35 \times 3 \cdot 65 + 3 \cdot 65 \times 3 \cdot 65$

(f) $5874 \times 5874 + 3774 \times 3774 - 7548 \times 5874$

(g) $\dfrac{7529 \times 7529 - 7519 \times 7519}{7529 + 7519}$

(h) $\dfrac{2345 \times 2345 - 759 \times 759}{2345 - 759}$

3. If $a - b = 4$ and $ab = 60$, what is the value of $a + b$?

4. If $a + b = 7$ and $ab = 12$, what is the value of $a - b$?

5. If $a + b = 9m$ and $ab = 18m^2$, what is the value of $a - b$?

6. If $x - y = 2$ and $xy = 63$, what is the value of $x^2 + y^2$?

7. If $x - \dfrac{1}{x} = 4$, prove that, $x^4 + \dfrac{1}{x^4} = 322$.

8. If $2x + \dfrac{2}{x} = 3$, what is the value of $x^2 + \dfrac{1}{x^2}$?

9. Sum total of an integer and its reciprocal is equal to 50.02. Find the product of fifth and sixth multiple of that integer.

10. Sum total of a natural number and its reciprocal is equal to 100.01. Find the product of fifth and seventh multiple of this number.

11. Half of a number and one fifth of its reciprocal are equal to 4.025. Find sum total of third, fourth and fifth multiple of that number.

12. Sum total of a number and its reciprocal is equal to 2. Find sum total of cube and square value of that number.

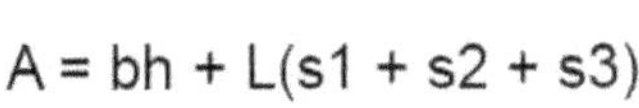

$$A = bh + L(s1 + s2 + s3)$$

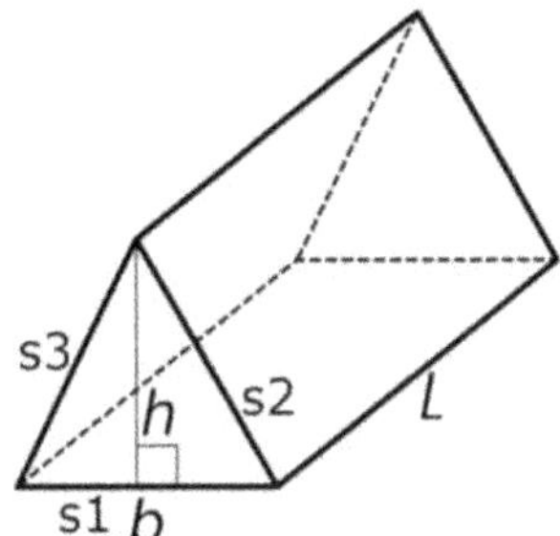

13. All measurements are in cm. Area is in square cm.

A	b	h	L	s1	s2	s3
....	12	8	60	12	10	10
....	6	4	20	6	5	5

14. If $x + \dfrac{2}{x} = 3$, what is the value of $x^3 + \dfrac{8}{x^3}$?

    (a) 1   (b) 8   (c) 9   (d) 16

15. Which one of the following is the factorized form of $p^4 + p^2 + 1$?

    (a) $(p^2 - p + 1)(p^2 + p - 1)$ (b) $(p^2 - p - 1)(p^2 + p + 1)$

    (c) $(p^2 + p + 1)(p^2 + p + 1)$ (d) $(p^2 + p + 1)(p^2 - p + 1)$

16. What are the factors of $x^2 - 5x + 4$?

    (a) $(x - 1), (x - 4)$ (b) $(x + 1), (x - 4)$

    (c) $(x + 2), (x - 2)$ (d) $(x - 5), (x - 1)$

17. What is the value of $(x - 7)(x - 5)$?

    (a) $x^2 + 12x + 35$ (b) $x^2 + 12x - 35$

    (c) $x^2 - 12x + 35$ (d) $x^2 - 12x - 35$

18. What is the value of $\dfrac{2\cdot9 \times 2\cdot9 - 1\cdot1 \times 1\cdot1}{2\cdot9 - 1\cdot1}$?

    (a) $1\cdot8$ (b) $1\cdot9$

    (c) 2   (d) 4

19. A number is increased by 20% and then further decreased by 20%. Find the total increase or decrease.

20. After selling six apples a shopkeeper made profit equal to the selling price of one apple. Find total profit in percentage.

Worksheet 3

01. Property Chart of Integers is given below: ...

(i) **Closure property:** Closure property is satisfied with respect to addition, subtraction and multiplication in the set of integers.

For a, b ∈ Z, a + b ∈ Z, a – b ∈ Z and a × b ∈ Z.

(ii) **Commutative property:** Commutative property is satisfied with respect to addition and multiplication in the set of integers.

If a, b ∈ Z, then a + b = b + a and a × b = b × a.

(iii) **Associative property:** Associative property is satisfied with respect to addition and multiplication in the set of integers.

If a, b, c ∈ Z, then

a + (b + c) = (a + b) + c = c + (b + a) and a × (b × c) = (a × b) × c = c × (b × a).

(iv) **Distributive property:** Multiplication is distributed over addition and subtraction in the set of integers.

For a, b and c ∈ Z, a (b + c) = ab + ac and a (b – c) = ab – ac.

(v) **Identity element:** 0 is the identity under addition and 1 is the identity under multiplication.

For a ∈ Z, a + 0 = a = 0 + a and a × 1 = a = 1 × a.

(vi) **Multiplication by zero:** For any integer a, a × 0 = 0 × a = 0.

Which Property can be used to calculate the following?

a) 101 X 99

b) 1002X 599 + 1002X 1

c) 121 X 0 X 1001 X 2004

d) 1021 + 989 + 2,009 + 1,991

e) 1,009 X 991

f) 2,081 X 1919 X 1,000

02. Prism: Surface Area

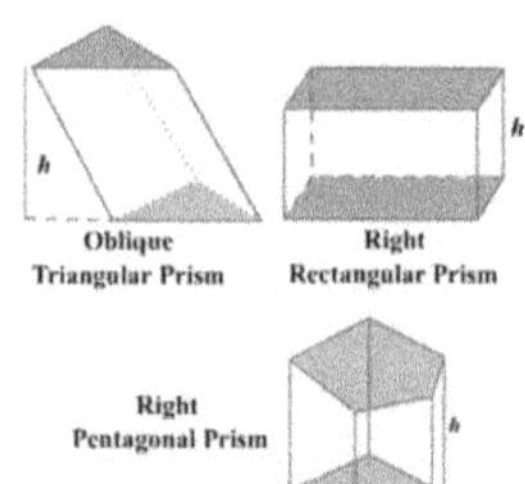

The lateral surface area of a prism is the sum of the areas of its lateral faces.
The total surface area of a prism is the sum of the areas of its lateral faces and its two bases.

The general formula for the lateral surface area of a right prism is L.S.A.=ph where p represents the perimeter of the base and h represents the height of the prism.

Calculate Total Surface Area and Lateral Surface Area of the following:..

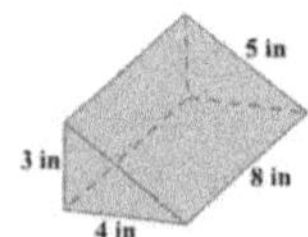

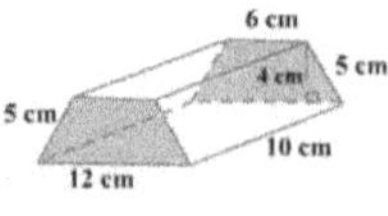

03: Radius of the flat surface of a cylinder is 7.7 cm. Length of this cylinder is 35 cm. Find its total surface area.

04. Solve the following:

Simplify (1 – 10) :

1. $\dfrac{3^3 \cdot 3^5}{3^6}$
   2. $\dfrac{5^3 \cdot 8}{2^4 \cdot 125}$
   3. $\dfrac{7^3 \times 7^{-3}}{3 \times 3^{-4}}$
   4. $\dfrac{\sqrt[3]{7^2} \cdot \sqrt[3]{7}}{\sqrt{7}}$

5. $(2^{-1} + 5^{-1})^{-1}$
   6. $(2a^{-1} + 3b^{-1})^{-1}$
   7. $\left(\dfrac{a^2 b^{-1}}{a^{-2} 6}\right)^2$

8. $\sqrt{x^{-1}y} \cdot \sqrt{y^{-1}z} \cdot \sqrt{z^{-1}x}, (x>0, y>0, z>0)$ 9. $\dfrac{2^{n+4} - 4 \cdot 2^{n+1}}{2^{n+2} \div 2}$ 10. $\dfrac{3^{m+1}}{(2^m)^{m-1}} \div \dfrac{3^{m+1}}{(3^{m-1})^{m+1}}$

Prove (11 – 18) :

11. $\dfrac{4^n - 1}{2^n - 1} = 2^n + 1$
    12. $\dfrac{2^{p+1} \cdot 3^{2p-q} \cdot 5^{p+q} \cdot 6^p}{6^q \cdot 10^{p+2} \cdot 15^q} = \dfrac{1}{50}$

13. $\left(\dfrac{a^{\ell}}{a^m}\right)^n \cdot \left(\dfrac{a^m}{a^n}\right)^{\ell} \cdot \left(\dfrac{a^n}{a^{\ell}}\right)^m = 1$
    14. $\dfrac{a^{p+q}}{a^{2r}} \times \dfrac{a^{q+r}}{a^{2p}} \times \dfrac{a^{r+p}}{a^{2q}} = 1$

15. $\left(\dfrac{x^a}{x^b}\right)^{\frac{1}{ab}} \cdot \left(\dfrac{x^b}{x^c}\right)^{\frac{1}{bc}} \cdot \left(\dfrac{x^c}{x^a}\right)^{\frac{1}{ca}} = 1$
    16. $\left(\dfrac{x^a}{x^b}\right)^{a+b} \cdot \left(\dfrac{x^b}{x^c}\right)^{b+c} \cdot \left(\dfrac{x^c}{x^a}\right)^{c+a} = 1$

17. $\left(\dfrac{x^p}{x^q}\right)^{p+q-r} \times \left(\dfrac{x^q}{x^r}\right)^{q+r-p} \times \left(\dfrac{x^r}{x^p}\right)^{r+p-q} = 1$

Example: Solve and write the solution set : $\dfrac{6x+1}{15} - \dfrac{2x-4}{7x-1} = \dfrac{2x-1}{5}$

Solution : $\dfrac{6x+1}{15} - \dfrac{2x-4}{7x-1} = \dfrac{2x-1}{5}$

or, $\dfrac{6x+1}{15} - \dfrac{2x-1}{5} = \dfrac{2x-4}{7x-1}$ [by transposition]

or, $\dfrac{6x+1-6x+3}{15} = \dfrac{2x-4}{7x-1}$ or, $\dfrac{4}{15} = \dfrac{2x-4}{7x-1}$

or, $15(2x-4) = 4(7x-1)$ [by cross multiplication]

or, $30x - 60 = 28x - 4$

or, $30x - 28x = 60 - 4$ [by transposition]

or, $2x = 56$,   or $x = 28$

$\therefore$ Solution is $x = 28$

and solution set is $S = \{28\}$.

05. Solve the following:

$$\dfrac{1}{x-3} + \dfrac{1}{x-4} = \dfrac{1}{x-2} + \dfrac{1}{x-5}$$

06. Find sets of solutions: $\sqrt{2x-3} + 5 = 2$

Worksheet 4

1: Complete the following chart.

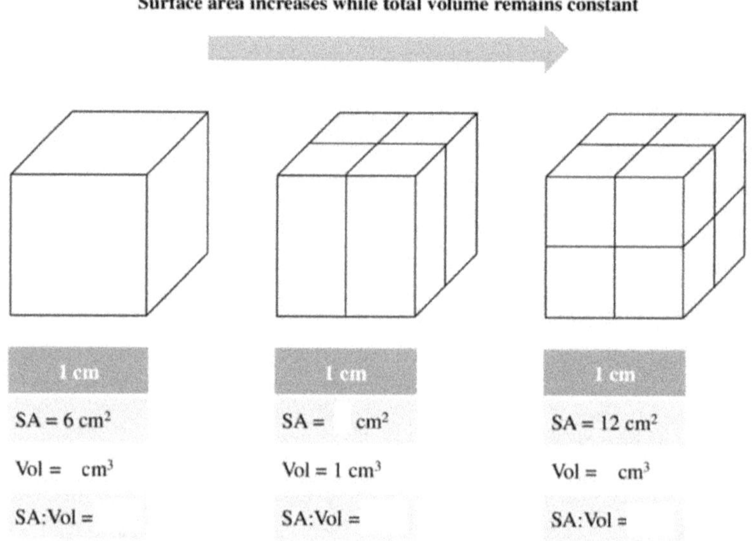

2. In a class if 4 students are seated in each bench, 3 benches remain vacant. But if 3 students are seated on each bench, 6 students are to remain standing. What is the number of students in that class ?

3. Sum of the digits of a number consisting of two digits is 9. If the number obtained by interchanging the places of the digits is less by 45 than the given number, what is the number ?

4. Number of passengers in a launch is 47 ; the fare per head for the cabin is twice that for the deck. The fare per head for the deck is $. 30. If the total fare collected is $. 1680, what is the number of passengers in the cabin ?

5. 120 coins of twenty five paisa and fifty paisa together is Rs. 35. What is the number of coins of each kind ?

6. A car passed over some distance at the speed of 60 km per hour and passed over the rest of the distance at the speed of 40 km per hour. The car passed over the total distance of 240 km in 5 hours. How far did the car pass over at the speed of 60 km per hour?

Quadratic Equation:

Equations of the form $ax^2 + bx + c = 0$ [where a, b, c are constants and $a \neq 0$] is called the quadratic equation with one variable. Left hand side of a quadratic equation is a polynomial of second degree, right hand side is generally taken to be zero.

Length and breadth of a rectangular region of area 12 square cm. are respectively x cm. and $(x-1)$ cm.

$\therefore$ area of the rectangular region is $= x(x-1)$ square cm.

By the question, $x(x-1) = 12$, or $x^2 - x - 12 = 0$.

x is the variable in the equation and highest power of x is 2.

Such equation is a quadratic equation. The equation, which has the highest degree 2 of the variable, is called the quadratic equation.

In class VIII, we have factorized the quadratic expressions with one variable of the forms $x^2 + px + q$ and $ax^2 + bx + c$. Here, we shall solve the equations of the forms $x^2 + px + q = 0$ and $ax^2 + bx + c = 0$ by factorizing the left hand side and by finding the value of the variable.

Example 1. Solve : $(x + 2)(x - 3) = 0$

Solution : $(x + 2)(x - 3) = 0$

$\therefore$ $x + 2 = 0$, or, $x - 3 = 0$

If $x + 2 = 0$, $x = -2$

Again, if $x - 3 = 0$, $x = 3$

$\therefore$ solution is $x = -2$ or, 3.

Example 2. Find the solution set : $y^2 = \sqrt{3}y$

Solution : $y^2 = \sqrt{3}y$

or, $y^2 - \sqrt{3}y = 0$ [By transposition, right hand side has been done zero]

or, $y(y - \sqrt{3}) = 0$

$\therefore$ $y = 0$, or $y - \sqrt{3} = 0$

If $y - \sqrt{3} = 0$, $y = \sqrt{3}$

$\therefore$ Solution set is $\{0, \sqrt{3}\}$.

Example 3. Solve and write the solution set : $x - 4 = \dfrac{x - 4}{x}, x \neq 0$.

Solution : $x - 4 = \dfrac{x - 4}{x}$

or, $x(x - 4) = x - 4$ [by cross-multiplication]

or, $x(x - 4) - (x - 4) = 0$ [by transposition]

or, $(x - 4)(x - 1) = 0$

$\therefore$ $x - 4 = 0$, or, $x - 1 = 0$

If $x - 4 = 0$, $x = 4$

Again, if $x - 1 = 0$, $x = 1$

$\therefore$ Solution is : $x = 1$ or, 4

and the solution set is $\{1, 4\}$.

7: Solve the following equation.

a) $11x^2 - 54x + 63$

b) $7x - 6x^2 + 20$

c) $3x^2 + 22x + 35$

d) $x^2 + 4y^2 - 4xy - 5x + 10y + 6$

Worksheet 5

1: Solve the following equation by using any suitable method.

a) $(x + 2)(x + 3) + (x - 3)(x - 2) - 2x(x + 1) = 0$

b) $\dfrac{x}{2} - \dfrac{4}{5} + \dfrac{x}{5} + \dfrac{3x}{10} = \dfrac{1}{5}$

c) $\dfrac{7}{x} + 35 = \dfrac{1}{10}$

2: Calculate...

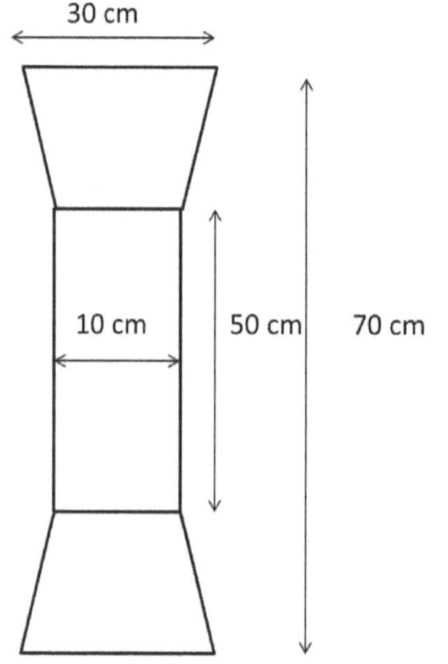

Find area of the figure depicted in the given diagram.

[Hints: Area of this shape will be equal to sum total of areas of two trapezium and a rectangle]

3: Top surface of a table resembles a trapezium in shape. Find its area if its parallel sides are 1 m and 1.2 m and perpendicular distance between them is 0.8 m.

4: The cross-section of a canal is a trapezium in shape. If the canal is 10 m wide at the top 6 m wide at the bottom and the area of cross-section is 72 m^2 determine its depth.

5: The area of a trapezium is 91 cm2 and its height is 7 cm. If one of the parallel sides is longer than the other by 8 cm, find the two parallel sides.

6: The area of a trapezium is 384 cm^2. Its parallel sides are in the ratio 3:5 and the perpendicular distance between them is 12 cm. Find the length of each one of the parallel sides.

7: Mishutka wants to buy a trapezium shaped field. Its side along the river is parallel and twice the side along the road. If the area of this field is 10,500 m^2 and the perpendicular distance between the two parallel sides is 100 m, find the length of the side along the river.

8: The parallel sides of a trapezium are 35 cm and 23 cm; its nonparallel sides are equal, each being 10 cm, find the area of the trapezium.

9: Statement about repeating decimal...

Repeating Decimal: A decimal in which a digit or set of digits repeat continuously is called a repeating or recurring or circulating or periodic decimal.

Examples: (i) $\frac{2}{3} - 0.66666...$

(ii) $\frac{5}{6} = 0.8333...$

(iii) $\frac{9}{11} = 0.81818181$

Period: The recurring part of a non-terminating, recurring decimal is called period.

Periodicity: The number of digits in the recurring part of the decimal is called its periodicity.

Examples: (i) In $\frac{2}{3} = 0.\overline{6}$, the period = 6; and the periodicity = 1.

(ii) In $\frac{13}{11} = 1.\overline{18}$, the period = 18; and the periodicity = 2.

Find Period and Periodicity of the following:

a) $\frac{3}{11}$ b) $\frac{11}{66}$ c) $\frac{99}{121}$ d) $\frac{111}{666}$ e) $\frac{199}{597}$

10: Is there any set of numbers having no definite position on the number line? Is there any definite location of the square root of (- 121) on the number line?

11: What least number can be added to the greatest number of six digits to make the value a perfect cube number?

12: Placing square roots on number line.

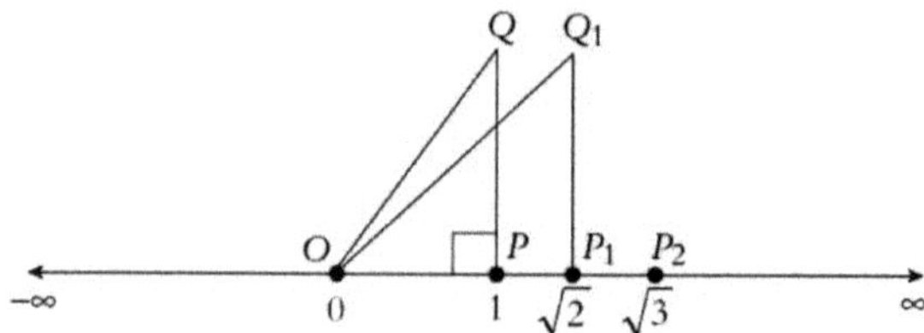

Draw the number line and mark point O at zero. Consider the points P and Q such that $OP = 1$ unit, $PQ = 1$ unit, and $PQ \perp OP$ as shown in the figure. From the right triangle OPQ,

$$OQ = \sqrt{OP^2 + PQ^2} = \sqrt{2} \ \text{Units}$$

Now with O as centre and $OQ = \sqrt{2}$ as radius, cut the number line at P_1.

$\Rightarrow OP_1 = \sqrt{2}$ which is an irrational number.

$\therefore P_1$ is a point on the number line corresponding to the irrational number $\sqrt{2}$.

By following such rules locate the square root of 5 on the number line.

13. Prime, C-prime and prime Triplets:

A number having only two factors are called Prime Numbers. A set of Prime numbers can be expressed differently.

Prime Triplets:

The set of three consecutive prime numbers is called a prime triplet.

Example: {3, 5, 7} is a prime triplet.

Co-prime:

Every pair of two natural numbers having no common factor, other than 1 is called a pair of co-primes. For example, consider the numbers 16 and 15.

A = set of factors of 16 = {1, 2, 4, 8, 16}

B = set of factors of 15 = {1, 3, 5, 15}

The common factor of 16 and 15 is 1 only.

Hence, they are relative primes.

These are denoted as (15, 16) = 1.

Co-Prime numbers are relatively Primes. Individually they may not be prime numbers.

Q 1: From the set {2, 3, 4, 5, 6, 7, 8, 9}, how many pairs of co-primes can be formed?
Q 2: Pamela wanted to type the first 290 whole numbers. Find the number of times he had to press the numbered keys.

[Number keys can be pressed 463 times if we type numbers from 1 to 190]

14: Sum total of first five Prime number is equal to ....

Worksheet 6

Euclid's Axioms and Postulates:

Euclid's axioms are given below:
1. A point is that which has no part.
2. A line has no end point.
3. A line has only length, but no breath and height.
4. A straight line is a line which lies evenly with the points on itself.
5. A surface is that which has length and breadth only.
6. The edges of a surface are lines.
7. A plane surface is a surface which lies evenly with the straight lines on itself.

Some of the axioms given by Euclid are:
(1) Things which are equal to the same thing are equal to one another.
(2) If equals are added to equals, the wholes are equal.
(3) If equals are subtracted from equals, the remainders are equal.
(4) Things which coincide with one another are equal to one another.
(5) The whole is greater than the part.
The five postulates of Euclid are:
Postulate 1: A straight line may be drawn from any one point to any other point.
Postulate 2: A terminated line can be produced indefinitely,
Postulate 3: A circle can be drawn with any center and any radius.
Postulate 4: All right angles are equal to one another.
Postulate 5: If a straight line falling on two straight lines makes the interior angles on the same side of it taken together less than two right angles, then the two straight lines, if produced indefinitely, meet on that side on which the sum of angles is less than two right angles.

1: "For two different points there exists one and only one straight line, on which both the points lie."
This statement corresponds to Postulate …..
2: Statements related to a set of geometrical rules:
(a) Space contains more than one plane.
(b) In each plane more than one straight lines lie.

(c) The points on a straight line and the real numbers can be related in such a way that every point on the line corresponds to a unique real number and conversely every real number corresponds to a unique point of the line.

All these rules are derived from Postulate ……..

Perfect Number:

A number for which sum of all its factors is equal to twice the number itself is called a perfect number.

Let us take some examples.

Euler proved that, if $2^k - 1$ is a prime number, then $2^{k-1}\left(2^k - 1\right)$ is a perfect number.

A perfect number can never be a prime number.

Example: (i) Consider the composite number 6.

Factors of 6 are 1, 2, 3, and 6.

Sum of factors $= (1 + 2 + 3 + 6) = 12$

Clearly, the sum of the factors of 6 is twice the number itself.

Hence, 6 is a perfect number.

(ii) Consider the composite number 48.

The set of factors of $48 = \{1, 2, 3, 4, 6, 8, 12, 16, 24, 48\}$

Sum of factors $= 1 + 2 + 3 + 4 + 6 + 8 + 12 + 16 + 24 + 48 = 124 \neq 2 \times 48$

Clearly, 48 is not a perfect number.

Q 3: Find out a set of five perfect numbers by following above mentioned process.

Q 4: Which of the following is/are a perfect number?

    12, 18, 6, 666, 606, 660

Q 5: Calculate area and outer boundary of the following.

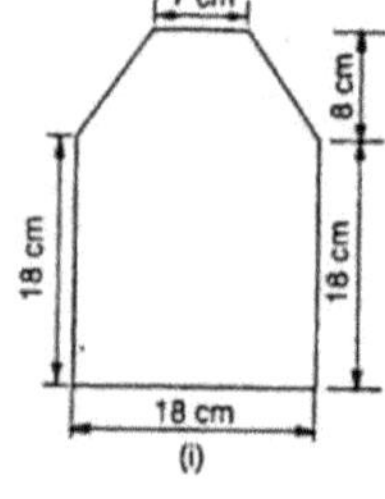

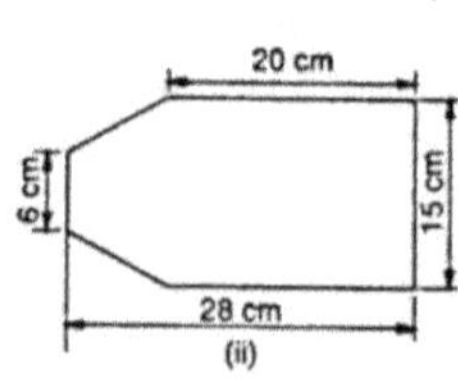

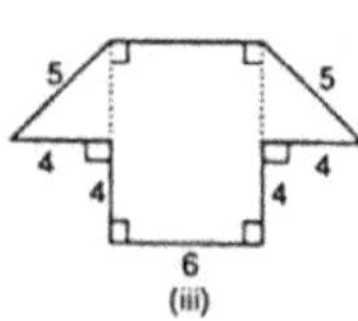

Q 6. What fraction of all the numbers from 1 to 66 are multiples of 6?

Q 7. Is there any pair of number having LCM 121 and HCF 36?

Q 8. How many prime factors will be there if we write 1331 in the form of a product of Prime factorisation?

Worksheet 7

Solve (1-10) :

1. $3(5x - 3) = 2(x + 2)$

2. $\dfrac{ay}{b} - \dfrac{by}{a} = a^2 - b^2$

3. $(z + 1)(z - 2) = (z - 4)(z + 2)$

4. $\dfrac{7x}{3} + \dfrac{3}{5} = \dfrac{2x}{5} - \dfrac{4}{3}$

5. $\dfrac{4}{2x + 1} + \dfrac{9}{3x + 2} = \dfrac{25}{5x + 4}$

6. $\dfrac{1}{x + 1} + \dfrac{1}{x + 4} = \dfrac{1}{x + 2} + \dfrac{1}{x + 3}$

7. $\dfrac{a}{x - a} + \dfrac{b}{x - b} = \dfrac{a + b}{x - a - b}$

8. $\dfrac{x - a}{b} + \dfrac{x - b}{a} + \dfrac{x - 3a - 3b}{a + b} = 0$

9. $\dfrac{x - a}{a^2 - b^2} = \dfrac{x - b}{b^2 - a^2}$

10. $(3 + \sqrt{3})z + 2 = 5 + 3\sqrt{3}.$

Find the solution set (11 - 19) :

11. $2x(x + 3) = 2x^2 + 12$

12. $2x + \sqrt{2} = 3x - 4 - 3\sqrt{2}$

13. $\dfrac{x + a}{x - b} = \dfrac{x + a}{x + c}$

14. $\dfrac{z - 2}{z - 1} = 2 - \dfrac{1}{z - 1}$

15. $\dfrac{1}{x} + \dfrac{1}{x + 1} = \dfrac{2}{x - 1}$

16. $\dfrac{m}{m - x} + \dfrac{n}{n - x} = \dfrac{m + n}{m + n - x}$

17. $\dfrac{1}{x + 2} + \dfrac{1}{x + 5} = \dfrac{1}{x + 4} + \dfrac{1}{x + 3}$

18. $\dfrac{2t - 6}{9} + \dfrac{15 - 2t}{12 - 5t} = \dfrac{4t - 15}{18}$

19. $\dfrac{x + 2b^2 + c^2}{a + b} + \dfrac{x + 2c^2 + a^2}{b + c} + \dfrac{x + 2a^2 + b^2}{c + a} = 0$

20. In a hypothetical sample of 20 people the amounts of money with them were found to be as follows:

114, 108, 100, 98, 101, 109, 117, 119, 126, 131, 136, 143, 156, 168, 182, 195, 207, 219, 235, 118.

Draw the histogram of the frequency distribution (taking one of the class intervals as 50-100).

21. What fraction of all the numbers starting from 1 to 1010 are multiples of 101?

22. Is there any pair of number having LCM 2662 and HCF 169?

23. …… X 25 X 40 X 125 = 10^{n}; Find the value of n.

Worksheet 8

1: Select correct options..

Statement 1:

When a transversal cuts two straight lines, such that

(a) pairs of corresponding angles are equal, or

(b) pairs of alternate interior angles are equal, or

(c) pairs of interior angles on the same side of the transversal are or equal to, the sum of two right angles the lines are parallel.

In the figure the line PQ intersects the straight lines AB and CD at E and F respectively and

(a) $\angle PEB$ = alternate $\angle EFD$

or, (b) $\angle AEF$ = Corresponding $\angle EFD$

or, (c) $\angle BEF + \angle EFD = 2$ right angles.

Therefore, the straight lines AB and CD are parallel.

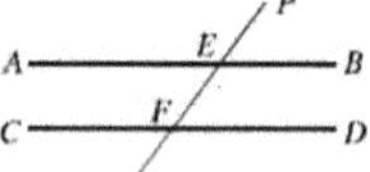

Statement 2: **The lines which are parallel to a given line are parallel to each other.**

Select correct option(s)

Options:

A: Statement 1 represents theorem and Statement 2 represents corollary.

B: Theorem and corollary support each other perfectly.

C: Modification is required in Statement 2.

D: Statement 1 is not supporting Statement 2.

2. The following figures are parallelograms. Find the degree values of the unknowns x, y, z.

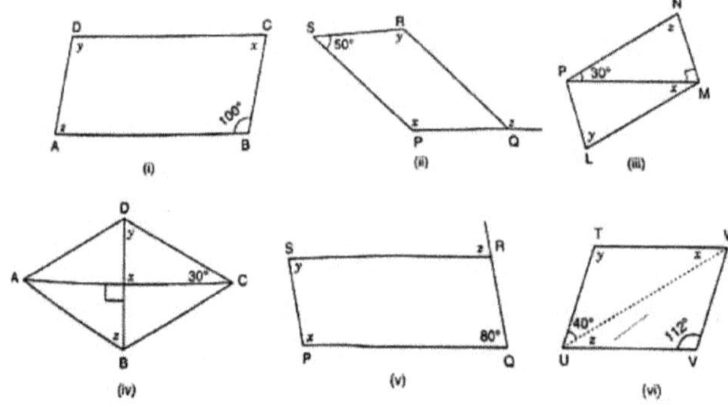

3: "All rectangles are special types of parallelogram, but all parallelograms are not rectangles." Is this statement true? Give reasons.

4. Sum total of all the interior angles of a pentagon is equal to …. times the sum total of all the interior angles of a triangle.

5. Diagram of different quadrilaterals:

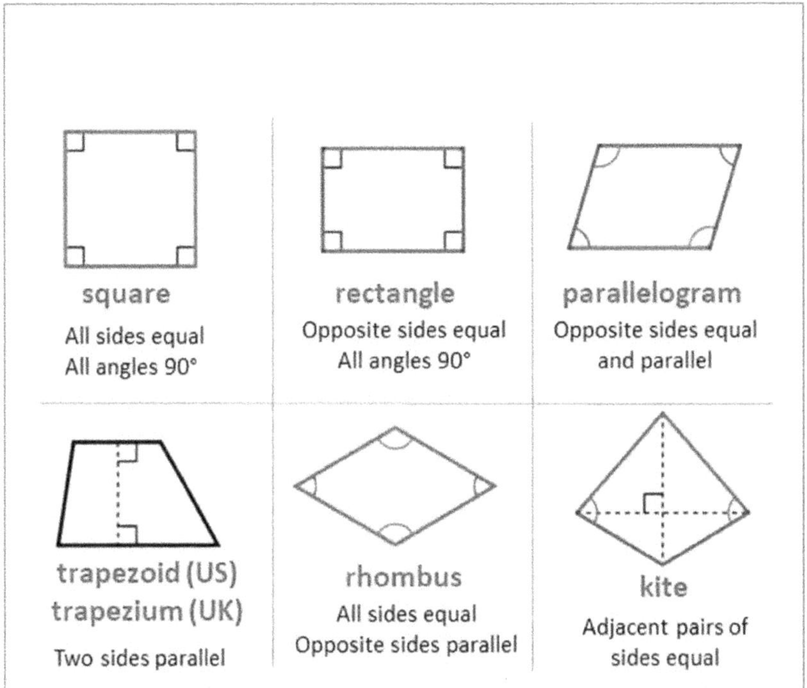

Statements:

I: Trapezoid cannot be considered as a parallelogram.

II: Rectangles can be considered as a special type of parallelogram.

III: Square is a special type of rectangle having length = breadth.

IV: Rhombus cannot be considered as a special type of parallelogram.

V: Kite is a special type of quadrilateral having adjacent pair of sides equal to each other.

VI: Rectangle and parallelogram have a common feature: Opposite sides are parallel to each other and also equal to each other.

Which of the above mentioned statement(s) cannot be considered as correct one?

6. In the following figures *GUNS* and *RUNS* are parallelograms. Find *x* and *y*.

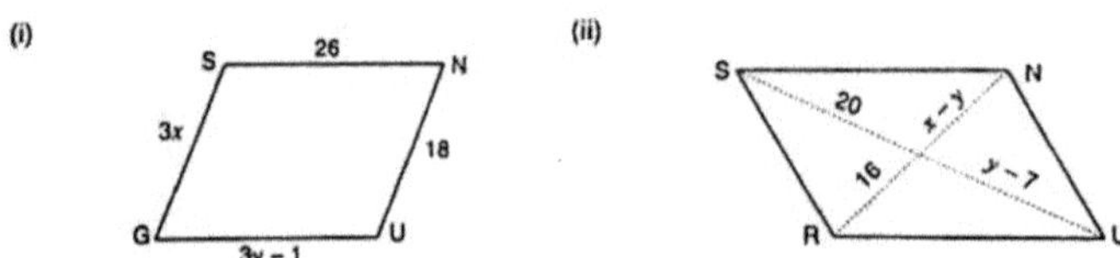

7. The measure of one angle of a parallelogram is 80°. What are the measures of the remaining angles?

8. Two adjacent angles of a parallelogram are as 2 : 3. Find the measures of all the angles of the parallelogram.

9. In a parallelogram ABCD, ∠D= 135°, determine the measure of ∠A and∠B .

10. The sum of two opposite angles of a parallelogram is 130°. Find all the angles of the parallelogram.

11. Select correct options : ...

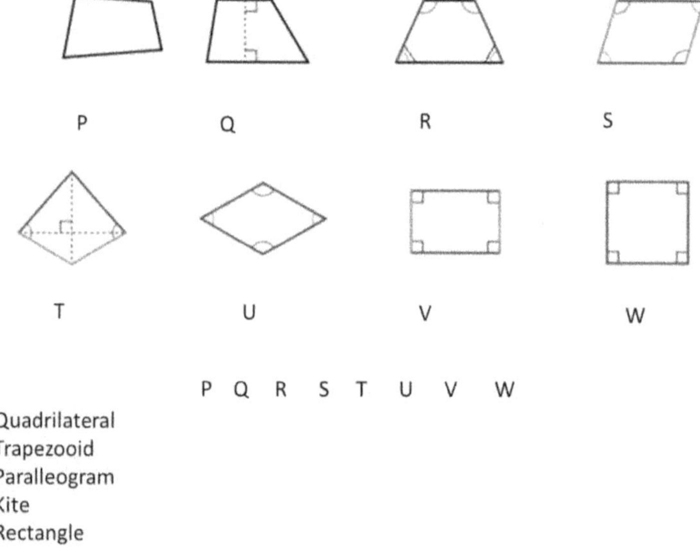

P   Q   R   S   T   U   V   W

Quadrilateral
Trapezooid
Paralleogram
Kite
Rectangle
Square

12. How many diagonals are there in a hexagon? Is there any relationship in between number of sides and number of diagonals of a polygon?

Worksheet 9

Q 1: Verify suggested response to the following problem by writing T for True and F for false.

Given below is a parallelogram *ABCD*. Complete each statement along with the definition or property used.

(i) *AD* = (ii) ∠*DCB*=

(iii) *OC* = (iv) ∠*DAB*+ ∠*CDA* =

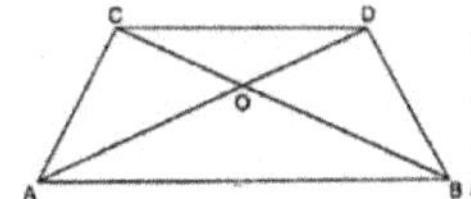

Suggested Response ..

(i) *AD* = BC [In a parallelogram diagonals bisect each other]

(ii) ∠*DCB* = ∠*BAD* [alternate interior angles are equal]

(iii) *OC* = OA [In a parallelogram diagonals bisect each other]

(iv) ∠*DAB*+ ∠*CDA* = 180° [Sum of adjacent angles in a parallelogram is 180°]

Q 2. Statements related to a polygon:

I.   The area of this shape is twice the area of a triangle created by any of its diagonals.

II.   The area of this shape is divided in half by any line passing through the midpoint.

III.   Any non-degenerate affine transformation takes this shape to another one.

IV.   This quadrilateral has rotational symmetry of order 2

V.   The sum of the distances from any interior point of this quadrilateral to the sides is independent of the location of the point.

Which of above mentioned property cannot satisfy the property of a parallelogram?

Q 3. "Parallelogram is a special type of a quadrilateral." Write at least three properties to satisfy the above mentioned statement.

Q 4. Two adjacent angles of a parallelogram are $(3x-4)°$ and $(3x+10)°$. Find the angles of the parallelogram.

Q 5. In a parallelogram ABCD, the diagonals bisect each other at O. If ∠ABC =30°, ∠BDC= 10° and ∠CAB =70°.

Find: ∠DAB, ∠ADC, ∠BCD, ∠AOD , ∠DOC, ∠BOC , ∠AOB , ∠ACD, ∠CAB, ∠ADB, ∠ACB, ∠DBC, and ∠DBA.

Q 6. The angle between the altitudes of a parallelogram, through the same vertex of an obtuse angle of the parallelogram is 60°. Find the angles of the parallelogram.

Q 7. Answer the following:

In Figure ABCD is a parallelogram, CE bisects ∠C and AF bisects ∠A. In each of the following, if the statement is true, give a reason for the same.

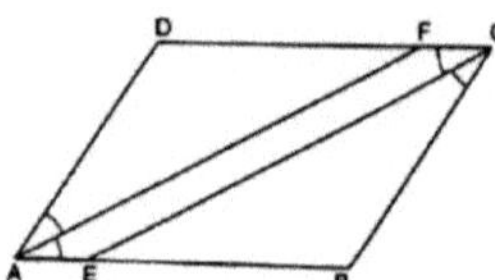

Q 8. Points E and F lie on diagonals AC of a parallelogram ABCD such that AE = CF. What type of quadrilateral is BFDE?

Q 9. In a parallelogram ABCD, AB = 10cm, AD = 6 cm. The bisector of ∠A meets DC in E, AE and BC produced meet at F. Find the length CF.

Q 10. Statements regarding a quadrilateral :

(i) It has two pairs of parallel sides.

(ii) It has two pairs of equal sides.

(iii) It has only two pairs of equal sides.

(iv) Two of its angles are at right angles.

(v) Its diagonals bisect each other at right angles.

(vi) Its diagonals are equal and perpendicular.

(vii) It has all its sides of equal lengths.

(viii) It is a parallelogram.

(ix) It is a quadrilateral.

(x) It can be a square.

(xi) It is a square.

This quadrilateral is a .... Which of the above mentioned statements related to rhombus are wrong?

Q 11. Complete the following statements:

(i) A rhombus is a parallelogram in which ________.

(ii) A square is a rhombus in which __________.

(iii) A rhombus has all its sides of _______ length.

(iv) The diagonals of a rhombus _____ each other at ______ angles.

(v) If the diagonals of a parallelogram bisect each other at right angles, then it is a ______.

Q 12. ABCD is a rhombus whose diagonals intersect at O . If AB =10 cm, diagonal BD = 16 cm, find the length of diagonal AC.

Q 13. The diagonal of a quadrilateral are of lengths 6 cm and 8 cm. If the diagonals bisect each other at right angles, what is the length of each side of the quadrilateral?

Q 14. Statements related to property of a rectangle are as follows:

(i) It has two pairs of equal sides.
(ii) It has all its sides of equal length.
(iii) Its diagonals are equal.
(iv) Its diagonals bisect each other.
(v) Its diagonals are perpendicular.
(vi) Its diagonals are perpendicular and bisect each other.
(vii) Its diagonals are equal and bisect each other.
(viii) Its diagonals are equal and perpendicular, and bisect each other.
(ix) All rectangles are squares.
(x) All rhombuses are parallelograms.
(xi) All squares are rhombuses and also rectangles.
(xii) All squares are not parallelograms.
Make needful corrections in the statements which are wrong.

Q 15. Complete the following statements:
(i) A ……………. is a parallelogram in which opposite sides are parallel and equal.
(ii) A ……………… is a rhombus in which all the sides are of equal length.
(iii) A ………………… is a rectangle in which opposite sides are equal and parallel and each angle is a right angle.

Q 16. The sides of a rectangle are in the ratio 6 : 5, and its perimeter is 44 cm. Find area of this rectangle. Draw the rectangle.
Q 17. The sides of a rectangle are in the ratio 4 : 5. Find its sides if the perimeter is 90 cm.
Q 18. Find the length of the diagonal of a rectangle whose sides are 12 cm and 5 cm.

Worksheet 10

1. Determine whether each of the following statements is true or false.
   a) $15^2 = 15 \times 15$ d) $81^2 = 2 \times 81$ g) $x^2 = 2^x$
   b) $20^2 = 20 \times 20$ e) $41 \times 41 = 41^2$ h) $x^2 = 2^{2x}$
   c) $19^2 = 19 \times 19$ f) $-(50)^2 = 2500$ i) $(-60)^2 = 3600$

2. Complete the following.
   a) $12 \times$ ______ $= 144$ d) $(3a)^2 =$ ____ $\times$ ____
   b) $51 \times$ ______ $= 2601$ e) $8a =$ ____ $+$ ____
   c) $60^2 =$ ____ $\times$ ____   f) $28 \times 28 =$ ______

3. Find the square of each of the following.
   a) 8   b) 12   c) 19   d) 51   e) 63   f) 100

4. Find x^2 in each of the following.

   a) $x = 6$ c) $x = -0.3$ e) $x = \dfrac{-50}{3}$ g) $x = 0.07$

   b) $x = \dfrac{1}{6}$ d) $x = -20$ f) $x = 56$

5. Difference between square values of two consecutive number of two digit is equal to 21. Find sum total of square values of both the numbers.

6. Is there any pair of number having LCM 3993 and HCF 169?

7. Find
   a) The 8th square number.   c) The first 12 square numbers.
   b) The 12th square number.

8. From the list given below indicate all numbers that are perfect squares.
   a) 50   20   64   30   1   80   8   49   9
   b) 10   21   57   4   60   125   7   27   48   16   25   90
   c) 137   150   75   110   50   625   64   81   144
   d) 90   180   216   100   81   75   140   169   125

9. Show that the difference between any two consecutive square numbers is an odd number.

10. Show that the difference between the 7th square number and the 4th square number is a multiple of 3.

Worksheet 11

1. Determine whether each of the following statements is true or false.

a) $\sqrt{0} = 0$

b) $\sqrt{25} = \pm 5$

c) $\sqrt{\dfrac{1}{4}} = \pm \dfrac{1}{2}$

d) $-\sqrt{121} = -11$

e) $-\sqrt{\dfrac{36}{324}} = \dfrac{1}{3}$

f) $\sqrt{\dfrac{324}{625}} = \dfrac{18}{25}$

g) $-\sqrt{\dfrac{900}{961}} = -\dfrac{30}{31}$

2. Find the square root of each of the following numbers.
   - a) 121
   - b) 144
   - c) 289
   - d) 361
   - e) 400
   - f) 441
   - g) 484
   - h) 529

3. Evaluate each of the following.

a) $\sqrt{\dfrac{1}{25}}$

b) $\sqrt{\dfrac{1}{81}}$

c) $-\sqrt{\dfrac{36}{144}}$

d) $-\sqrt{576}$

e) $\dfrac{\sqrt{529}}{\sqrt{625}}$

f) $-\sqrt{676}$

g) $\sqrt{729}$

h) $-\sqrt{784}$

i) $\sqrt{\dfrac{16}{25}}$

Note: If a number y > 0 is the square of a positive number x (x > 0), then the number x is called the square root of y.

It can be written as $y = x^2$; or $x = \sqrt{y}$

4:

Worksheet 12

1. Square root of a number exceeds the greatest four digit number by 1. Find the sum total of cube and square value of that number.

2. Simplify the following:

a) $\sqrt{0.25}$

b) $\sqrt{0.0625}$

c) $\sqrt{\dfrac{1296}{1024}}$

d) $\sqrt{\dfrac{625}{1024}}$

e) $\sqrt{\dfrac{81}{324}}$

f) $\sqrt{\dfrac{144}{400}}$

3. Simplify a) $\sqrt{625-0}-\sqrt{172-3}$

b) $\sqrt{81\times625}$

c) $\sqrt{\left(\dfrac{1}{64}\right)^2}$

4. Does every number have two square roots? Explain.

5. Which of the following are perfect squares?

{0, 1, 4, 7, 12, 16, 25, 30, 36, 42, 49}

6. Which of the following are perfect squares?

{50, 64, 72, 81, 95, 100, 121, 140, 144, 169}

7. Copy and complete.

a) $3^2 + 4^2 + 12^2 = 13^2$

b) $5^2 + 6^2 + \underline{\quad} = \underline{\quad}$

c) $6^2 + 7^2 + \underline{\quad} = \underline{\quad}$

d) $x^2 + (x+1)^2 + \underline{\quad} = \underline{\quad}$

8. Sum total of square values of three consecutive numbers is equal to 245. Find sum total of square value and cube value of the greatest number.

9. $x^3 + x^2 + x = 14$. Find the value of $[(x+1)^2 - (x-1)^2]$.

10. What fraction of all the numbers starting from 1 to 100 are square numbers?

11. What fraction of all the numbers starting from 1 to 100 are cube numbers?

12. Sum total of square and cube value of a natural number is 36. Find the number.

Worksheet 13

I: Answer the following.

1. Determine whether each of the following statements is true or false.

   a) $4^3 = 16 \times 4$ c) $(-3)^3 = 27$ e) $\left(\dfrac{4}{3}\right)^3 = \dfrac{64}{125}$

   b) $4^3 = 64$ d) $\left(\dfrac{3}{4}\right)^3 = \dfrac{27}{16}$ f) $\sqrt[3]{64} = 4$

2. Find x^3 in each of the following.

   a) $x = 8$ c) $x = -4$ e) $x = \dfrac{-1}{5}$

   b) $x = 0.4$ d) $x = -\dfrac{1}{4}$ f) $x = -0.2$

3. Find the approximate values of x^3 in each of the following.
   a) $x = -2.49$ c) $x = 2.98$
   b) $x = 2.29$ d) $x = 0.025$

4. The dimensions of a cuboid are
   4xcm, 6xcm and 10xcm. Find
   a) The total surface area
   b) The volume

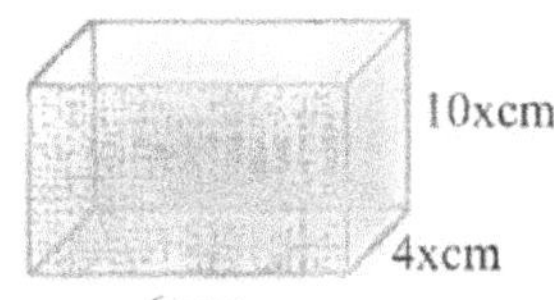

II. Study the pattern and find a, b, c and d.

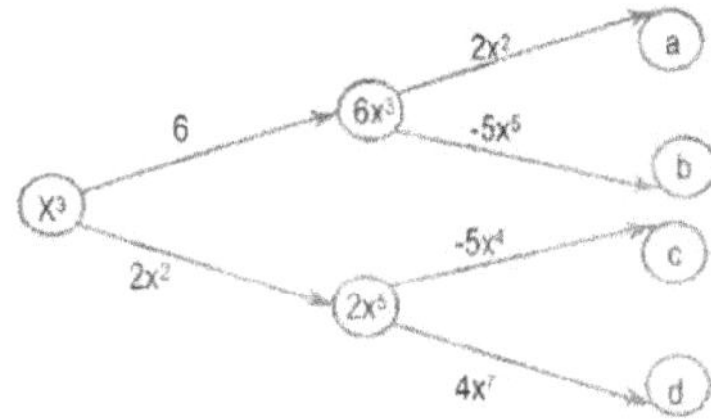

III. An amoeba is a single cell animal. When
the cell splits by a process called "fission"
there are then two animals. In a few hours
a single amoeba can become a large
colony of amoebas as shown to the right.

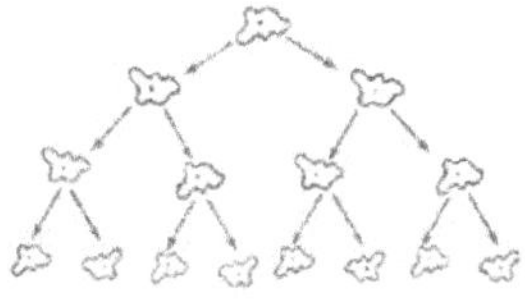

III: Read the passage and answer the questions as follows.

Read the following and select correct options ....

Natural Number

1, 2, 3, 4......... etc. numbers are called natural number or positive whole numbers. 2, 3, 5, 7......... etc. are prime numbers and 4, 6, 8, 9,......... etc. are composite numbers.

Integers

All numbers (both positive and negative) with zero (0) are called integers i.e. .... $-3, -2, -1, 0, 1, 2, 3$......... etc. are integers.

Fractional Number

If p, q are co-prime numbers ; $q \neq 0$ and $q \neq 1$, numbers expressed in $\dfrac{p}{q}$ form are called fractional number.

Example : $\dfrac{1}{2}, \dfrac{3}{2}, \dfrac{-5}{3}$ etc. are fractional numbers.

If $p < q$, then it is a proper fraction and if $p > q$ then it is an improper fraction :

Example $\dfrac{1}{2}, \dfrac{1}{3}, \dfrac{2}{3}, \dfrac{1}{4},$ .... etc. proper and $\dfrac{3}{2}, \dfrac{4}{3}, \dfrac{5}{3}, \dfrac{5}{4},$ ..... etc. improper fraction.

Rational Number

If p and q are integers and $q \neq 0$, number expressed in the form $\dfrac{p}{q}$ is called rational number. For example : $\dfrac{3}{1} = 3, \dfrac{11}{2} = 5.5, \dfrac{5}{3} = 1.666...$ etc. are rational numbers.

Select Correct options...

	Integer	Fraction	Rational Number

a) -102

b) 10.101

c) 11.102

d) -101.101

e) $11\dfrac{11}{101}$

f) $\sqrt{-121}$

g) $\sqrt[3]{1331}$

IV: Which of the following options is not correct?

A: All integers are rational numbers.

B: Non-terminating repeated decimals cannot be expressed in the form of any rational number.

C: All whole numbers can be expressed in the form of equivalent rational numbers having non-zero denominators.

D: Numerator and denominator of a proper fraction at its simplest form are co-rime numbers.

Worksheet 14

I: Study the property of Irrational number and Decimal Fractional Numbers ...

Irrational Number

Numbers which cannot be expressed in $\dfrac{p}{q}$ form, where p, q are integers and $q \neq 0$ are called Irrational Numbers. Square root of a number which is not perfect square, is an irrational number. For example: $\sqrt{2} = 1.414213......$, $\sqrt{3} = 1.732.....$, $\dfrac{\sqrt{5}}{2} = 1.58113....$ etc. are irrational numbers. Irrational number cannot be expressed as the ratio of two integers.

Decimal Fractional Number

If rational and irrational numbers are expressed in decimal, they are known as decimal fractional numbers. As for instance, $3 = 3 \cdot 0, \dfrac{5}{2} = 2 \cdot 5, \dfrac{10}{3} = 3 \cdot 3333......., \sqrt{3} = 1 \cdot 732.........$ etc. are decimal fractional numbers. After the decimal, if the number of digits are finite, it is terminating decimals and if it is infinite it is known as non-terminating decimal number. For example, 0.52, 3.4152 etc. are terminating decimals and $1 \cdot 333......., 2 \cdot 123512367..........$ etc. are non-terminating decimals. Again, if the digits after the decimal of numbers are repeated among themselves, they are known recurring decimals and if they are not repeated, they are called non-recurring decimals. For example : $1 \cdot 2323........., 5 \cdot 6\dot{5}\dot{4}$ etc. are the the recurring decimals and $0 \cdot 523050056........, 2 \cdot 12340314........$ etc. are non-recurring decimals.

Real Number

All rational and irrational numbers are known as real numbers. For example :

$0, \pm 1, \pm 2, \pm 3,.......... \quad \pm \dfrac{1}{2}, \pm \dfrac{3}{2}, \pm \dfrac{4}{3},......... \quad \sqrt{2}, \sqrt{3}, \sqrt{5}, \sqrt{6}......$

$1 \cdot 23, 0 \cdot 415, 1 \cdot 3333......., 0 \cdot \dot{6}\dot{2}, 4 \cdot 120345061..........$ etc. are real numbers.

Positive Number

All real numbers greater than zero are called positive numbers. As for instance

$1, 2, \dfrac{1}{2}, \dfrac{3}{2}, \sqrt{2}, 0 \cdot 415, 0 \cdot \dot{6}\dot{2}, 4 \cdot 120345061..............$ etc. are positive numbers.

Negative Number

All real numbers less than zero are called negative numbers. For example, $-1, -2, -\dfrac{1}{2}, -\dfrac{3}{2}, -\sqrt{2}, -0 \cdot 415, -0 \cdot \dot{6}\dot{2}, -4 \cdot 120345061..............$ etc. are

Select the option which is/are correct.

A: Square root of a negative integer cannot be expressed in the form of rational number.

B: All non-continuing repeating type decimals can be expressed in the form of a rational number.

II. A boatman can go x km in time 1 t hour against the current. To cover that distance along the current he takes 2 t hour. How much is the speed of the boat and the current.

III: A pipe can fill up an empty tank in 12 minutes. Another pipe flows out 14 litre of water per minute. If the two pipes are opened together and the empty tank is filled up in 96 minutes, how much water does the tank contain?

IV: Solve the following.

1. Find $\dfrac{3}{7}+\left(\dfrac{-6}{11}\right)+\left(\dfrac{-8}{21}\right)+\dfrac{5}{22}$

2. Find $\dfrac{-4}{5}\times\dfrac{3}{7}\times\dfrac{15}{16}\times\left(\dfrac{-14}{9}\right)$

3. Find using distributive property: $(i)\left\{\dfrac{7}{5}\times\left(\dfrac{-3}{12}\right)\right\}+\left\{\dfrac{7}{5}\times\dfrac{5}{12}\right\}$ $(ii)\left\{\dfrac{9}{16}\times\dfrac{4}{12}\right\}+\left\{\dfrac{9}{16}\times\dfrac{-3}{9}\right\}$

4. Find $\dfrac{2}{5}\times\dfrac{-3}{7}-\dfrac{1}{14}-\dfrac{3}{7}\times\dfrac{3}{5}$

5. Simplify: $\dfrac{-4}{5}\times\dfrac{3}{7}\times\dfrac{15}{16}\times\left(\dfrac{-14}{9}\right)$

6. Multiply $\dfrac{6}{13}$ by the reciprocal of $\dfrac{-7}{16}$.

7. What number should be added to $\dfrac{7}{12}$ to get $\dfrac{4}{15}$?

8. What number should be subtracted from $-\dfrac{3}{5}$ to get –2?

9. Is $\dfrac{8}{9}$ the multiplicative reciprocal of $-1\dfrac{1}{8}$? Why or why not?

10. Is 0.3 the multiplicative reciprocal of $3\dfrac{1}{3}$? Why or why not?

11. Write any 3 rational numbers between –2 and 0.

12. Find any ten rational numbers between $\dfrac{-5}{6}$ and $\dfrac{5}{8}$

13. Find three rational numbers between $\dfrac{1}{4}$ and $\dfrac{1}{2}$

14. Find ten rational numbers between $\dfrac{1}{4}$ and $\dfrac{1}{2}$

15. Represent these numbers on the number line. $(i)\dfrac{7}{4}(ii)\dfrac{-5}{6}(iii)\dfrac{4}{7}(iv)\dfrac{9}{4}$

16. Represent $\dfrac{-2}{11},\dfrac{-5}{11},\dfrac{-9}{11}$ on the number line

V: Write a rational number that does not have reciprocal.

VI: Sum total of square of a number and reciprocal of that number is equal to 16.25. Find sum total of cube and square value of that number.

Worksheet 15

1. Simplify: $\left(\frac{11}{23} \times \frac{46}{33} \times \frac{29}{61} \times \frac{122}{87}\right) \times 64$

2. Verify that $(x \times y)^{-1} = x^{-1} \times y^{-1}$ when $x = \frac{-2}{3}$ and $y = \frac{-3}{5}$

3. If you subtract $\frac{1}{2}$ from a number and multiply the result by $\frac{1}{2}$, you get $\frac{1}{8}$. What is the number?

4. Three consecutive integers are such that when they are taken in increasing order and multiplied by 2, 3, and 4 respectively, they add up to 74. Find these numbers.

5. Represent the following rational numbers on the number line
   (a) $-\frac{1}{4}$ (b) $-1\frac{1}{5}$ (c) $-3\frac{8}{5}$

6. Represent the following rational numbers on the number line
   (a) $-\frac{7}{10}$ (b) $-5\frac{3}{5}$.

7. Find two rational numbers between (i) -2 and 2. (ii) -1 and 0.

8. Insert six rational numbers between (i) $-\frac{1}{3}$ and $-\frac{2}{3}$ (ii) $\frac{1}{4}$ and $\frac{1}{2}$.

9. Arrange the following numbers in ascending order: $\frac{4}{-9}, \frac{-5}{12}, \frac{7}{-18}, \frac{-2}{3}$

10. Arrange the following numbers in descending order: $-\frac{5}{6}, -\frac{7}{12}, \frac{-13}{28}, \frac{23}{-24}$

11. Represent $4\frac{2}{3}$ on the number line.

12. What number should be added to $\frac{-7}{8}$ to get $\frac{4}{9}$?

13. The sum of two rational numbers is $\frac{-1}{2}$. If one of the numbers is $\frac{5}{6}$, find the other.

14. What number should be subtracted from $\frac{-2}{3}$ to get $\frac{-1}{2}$?

15. Divide the sum of $\frac{13}{5}$ and $\frac{-12}{7}$ by the product of $\frac{-31}{7}$ and $\frac{-1}{2}$.

16. The product of two rational numbers is $\frac{-16}{9}$. If one of the numbers is $\frac{-4}{3}$, find the other.

17. Find three rational numbers between 4 and 5.

18. Find three rational numbers between $\frac{2}{3}$ and $\frac{3}{4}$.

19. Find four rational numbers between 3/7 and 5/11.

20.

..

Worksheet 16

1. Explain why the terms $4x$ and $4x^2$ are not like terms.

2. Explain why the terms $14w^3$ and $14z^3$ are not like terms.

3. Categorize the following expressions as a monomial, a binomial or a trinomial.

   a. 26

   b. $50\,bc^2$

   c. $90 + x$

   d. $16x^2$

   e. $10a^2 + 5a$

   f. $27x + \dfrac{3}{2}$

   g. $20w^4 - 10w^2$

   h. $2t - 10t^4 - 10a$

   i. $70z + 13z^2 - 16$

4. Work out the value of these algebraic expressions using the values given.

   a. $2(a + 3)$ if $a = 5$

   b. $4(x + y)$ if $x = 5$ and $y = -3$

   c. $\dfrac{7 \cdot x}{y}$ if $x = -3$ and $y = -2$

   d. $\dfrac{2a + b}{c}$ if $a = 3$, $b = 4$ and $c = 2$

   e. $2(b + c)^2 - 3(b - c)^2$ if $b = 8$ and $c = -4$

   f. $(a + b)^2 + (a + c)^2$ if $a = 2$, $b = 8$ and $c = -4$

   g. $c(a + b)^3$ if $a = 3$, $b = 5$ and $c = 40$

5. Solve for d if $d = \sqrt{(x_2 - x_1)^2 + (y_2 - y_1)^2}$ if $x_1 = 3$, $y_1 = 4$ and $x_2 = 12$, $y_2 = 37$.

6. $y\dfrac{[3x + 6y(x-20)]}{2x + 12}$ if $x = 5$ and $y = \dfrac{1}{2}$

7. Collect like terms together.

   a. $xy + ab - cd + 2xy - ab + dc$

   b. $3x^2 + 4x + 6 - x^2 - 3x - 3$

   c. $3y^2 - 6x + y^2 + x^2 + 7x + 4x^2$

   d. $5 + 2y + 3y^2 - 8y - 6 + 2y^2 + 3$

   e. $6x^2 - 7x + 8 - 3x^2 + 5x - 10$

   f. $2x^2 - 3x + 8 + x^2 + 4x + 4$

8. Sum total of a number and quarter of its reciprocal is equal to 4.0625. If we take the number as x, then find the value of $x^3 + x^2 + x$.

9. There is equal number of students in each row. Number of rows is also equal to the number of students in each row. If total number of students in the parade ground is equal to 12321, then find the number of students in each row.

10. The length of the sides of a cubes is related to the volume of the cube according to the formula: $x = \sqrt[3]{V}$.

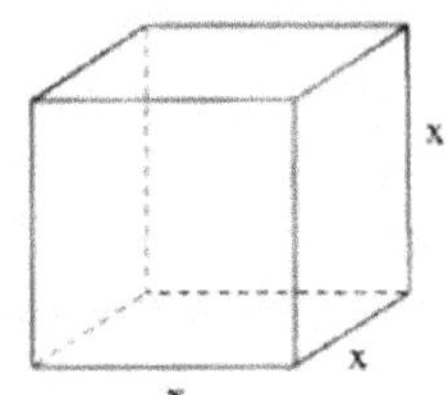

a) What is the volume of the cube if the side length is 25cm.

b) What is the volume of the cube if the side length is 40 cm.

11. In Figure **2** to the right find:

a) the surface area of a cube.

b) the volume of a cube.

c) compare the surface area and the volume of a given a cube

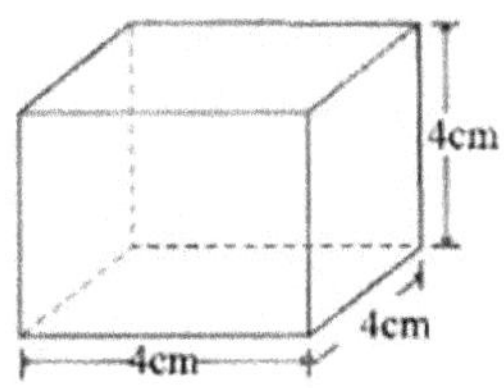

Figure 2

12. Prove that the difference of the square of an even number is multiple of 4.

13. Show that 64 can be written as either 2^6 or 4^3.

14. Look at this number pattern.

$7^2 = 49$

$67^2 = 4489$

$667^2 = 444889$

$6667^2 = 44448889$

This pattern continues.

a) Write down the next line of the pattern.

b) Use the pattern to work out 6666667^2.

15. Find three consecutive square numbers whose sum is 149.

16. Find the square root of $25x^2 - 40xy + 16y^2$.

17. Find the square root of $\dfrac{64a^2}{9b^2} + 4 + \dfrac{32a}{3b}$.

18. Find square root of 0.0625.

19. $\sqrt[4]{0.0064} = x$; Find the value of $x^4 + x^3 + x^2 + x^{-1} + x^{-2}$

20. $\sqrt[5]{3125} + \sqrt[4]{0.0064} + \sqrt[3]{0.729} - x$; Find the value of $\dfrac{1}{x^2} + \dfrac{1}{x^3} + \dfrac{1}{x^{-1}} + x$

21. Sum total of three consecutive square number is 29. Find the numbers.

22. When twice a non-zero positive number is divided by its cube root, the quotient is obtained as 32. If the cube of the number is divided by the number itself, then the quotient is ______.

Worksheet 17

1. When a number is multiplied by itself, the product is said to be _______ of that number.

2. The number of zeroes at the end of the square of a number is _______ the number of zeroes at the end of the number.

3. When a 'n' digit number is squared, then the number of digits in the square, thus, obtained is _______.

4. If $7^2 = 49$ and $0.7^2 = 0.49$, then $0.007^2 =$ _______.

5. The smallest number with which 16 should be multiplied to make it a perfect cube is _______.

6. The cube root of 125 is _______.

7. The square of a proper fraction is always _______ than itself.

8. The square of an odd number is always odd. Is the given statement true?

9. The square of a prime number is always prime. Is the given statement true?

10. The square root of a 4 digit or a 3 digit (perfect square) number is a _______ digit number.

11. If the units digit of a number is 2, then it does not have a square root. Is the given statement true?

12. If the units digit of a perfect square is 5, then the units digit of its square root is _______.

13. The square root of a prime number can be obtained approximately but not exactly. Is the given statement true?

14. If x is a non-zero number, then $x \times x \times x$, written as _______ is called the _______ of x.

15. A number n is a perfect cube only if there is an integer m such that $n =$ _______.

16. The smallest number by which 81 should be divided to make it a perfect cube is _______.

17. The cubes of the digits 1, 4, 5, 6, and 9 are the numbers ending in the same digits 1, 4, 5, 6, and 9, respectively (True/False).

18. Cubes of the numbers for which the digits in the units place are 2, 8 and 3, 7 ends in _______ and _______, respectively.

19. If a number ends in two 9's, then its cube ends in _______ number of 9's.

20. What is the digit in the units place of the cube of 31?

21. Number of digits in the cube of a two-digit number may be _______.

22. Cube root of a perfect even cube is _______ and the perfect odd cube is _______.

23. The cube root of $\dfrac{27}{8}$ is _______.

24. $3\sqrt[3]{\dfrac{3.43}{10}} =$ _______

25. $\sqrt[3]{a^6 \times b^9} =$ _______

26. The cube root of (-125) is _______.

27. 216 is the cube of _______.

28. If m is a cube root of n, then we write $m =$ _______.

29. $\sqrt[3]{0.125} + \sqrt[3]{0.729} =$ _______

30. $\sqrt[3]{-m^6} =$ _______

31. There is certain number of rows of chairs in a room. The number of chairs in each row is thrice the total number of rows. Find the number of chairs in each row and number of rows in the room if the total number of chairs is 2187.

32. In a five-digit number 1b6a3, then a is the greatest single-digit perfect cube and twice of it exceeds b by 7. Then the sum of the number and its cube root is _____.

33. Find the divisor and the quotient, given the dividend is 1035, the divisor is one-fourth the quotient, and the remainder is 11.

34. The smallest number which must be subtracted from 3400 to make it a perfect cube is _____.

35. The least positive integer with which 661.25 should be multiplied so that the product is a perfect square is _______.

36. Answer the following:

1. The least 4 digit number which is a perfect square is __________.

   (a) 1024   (b) 1016

   (c) 1036   (d) 1044

2. An odd number when multiplied by itself gives 2401. Find the number.

   (a) 41   (b) 39

   (c) 49   (d) 51

3. If the units digit of a perfect square is 4, then the units digit of its square root can be __________.

   (A) 2   (B) 8

   (a) Only (A)   (b) Only (B)

   (c) Either (A) or (B)   (d) Neither (A) nor (B)

4. What will be the units digit of the squares of the following numbers?

   (A) 71   (B) 669

   (C) 2533   (D) 30,827

   (a) 1   (b) 9

   (c) Both (a) and (b)   (d) 8

5. Which of the following is not a perfect square?

   (a) 12,544   (b) 3136

   (c) 23,832   (d) 1296

6. The smallest number with which 120 should be multiplied, so that the product is a perfect square is __________.

   (a) 120   (b) 60

   (c) 30   (d) 15

7. The greatest 3-digit number which is a perfect square is __________.

   (a) 729   (b) 927

   (c) 961   (d) 972

8. If p and q are perfect squares, then $\sqrt{\dfrac{p}{q}}$ is always a rational number. Is the statement true?

9. $\sqrt[3]{\dfrac{-a^6 \times b^3 \times c^{21}}{c^9 \times a^{12}}} =$ __________.

   (a) $\dfrac{-bc^3}{a^2}$ (b) $\dfrac{bc^4}{a^2}$

   (c) $\dfrac{-ab^4}{c^2}$ (d) $\dfrac{-bc^4}{a^2}$

10. If $3(x - 2)^2 = 507$, then x can be __________.

    (a) 13   (b) 12

    (c) 15   (d) 14

11. The value of $\sqrt{117^2 - 108^2}$ is __________.

    (a) 55   (b) 45

    (c) 35   (d) 65

12. The square root of $\dfrac{36}{5}$ when corrected to two decimal places is __________.

    (a) 2.68   (b) 2.69

    (c) 2.67   (d) 2.66

13. If the product of two equal numbers is 1444, then the numbers are __________.

    (a) 48, 48   (b) 38, 38

    (c) 32, 32   (d) 42, 42

14. The cube of the number p is 16 times the number. Then find p where $p \neq 0$ and $p \neq -4$.

    (a) 4   (b) 3

    (c) 8   (d) 2

15. The cube of a number x is nine times of x, then find x, if $x \neq 0$ and $x \neq -3$.

    (a) 8   (b) 2

    (c) 4   (d) 3

16. The digit in the units place for the cube of a four-digit number of the form $xyz8$ is __________.

    (a) 8   (b) 4

    (c) 2   (d) Cannot say

37. A man purchased a plot which is in the shape of a square. The area of the plot is 12 hectares 3201 m^2. Find the length of each side of the plot (in m).

38. A certain number of men went to a hotel. Each of them spent as many rupees as one-fourth of the men. If the total bill paid was Rs. 20,449, then how many men visited the hotel?

39. The unit's digit of the square of a number and the units digit of the cube of the number are equal to the units digit of the number. How many values are possible for the unit's digits of such numbers?

40. The unit's digit of the square root of a number and the units digit of the cube root of the number is equal to the units digit of the number. How many values are possible for the unit's digits of such numbers?

41. $\sqrt[3]{1+2+3+\cdots.+51} =$ ....

42. $\sqrt{x} + \dfrac{58}{\sqrt{x}} = 31.\,Find\ the\ value\ of\ (x+4)^2$

43. Statement about Radicals:

A number x which is such that the product of two x's is b is denoted by $\sqrt[2]{b}$ or $\sqrt{b}$.

Example: $2 = \sqrt{4}$

$3 = \sqrt{9}$

The number x which is such that the product of three x's is b is denoted by $\sqrt[3]{b}$.

Example: $2 = \sqrt[3]{8}$

$3 = \sqrt[3]{27}$

In general, the number x which is such that the product of n x's is b is denoted as $\sqrt[n]{b}$ and read as the nth root of b. Here, n may be any positive integer. $\sqrt[n]{b}$ is called a **radical**.

The sign $\sqrt[n]{\ }$ is called the **radical sign**. The number n, inside the radical sign in smaller size, is called the **index** of the radical. In this class, we shall consider only the positive integral values of the index. The number under the radical sign is called the **radicand**. The operation of finding the nth root of a number is called root extraction or evolution. Evolution is the inverse of involution.

If $n = 2$ or 3, then the expression $\sqrt[n]{b}$ is more commonly called the square root of b and cube root of b, respectively.

Example: For $\sqrt[3]{125} = 5$, 3 is the index of the radical, 125 is the radicand, and 5 is the cube root of 125.

We have defined the nth root of a number b as a number which has a certain property. Two consequences follow from this definition.

Complete the following:

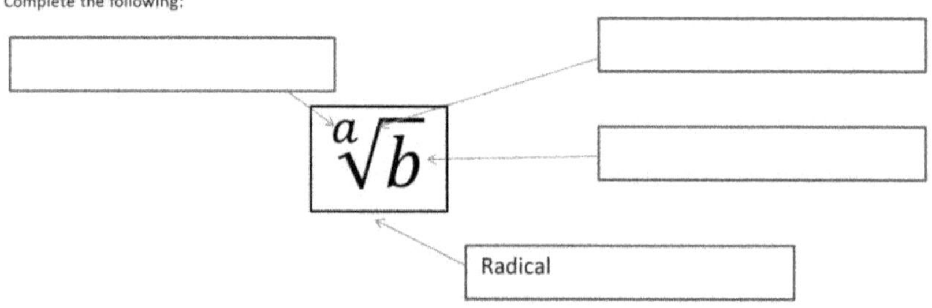

44. If $x^{\frac{-p}{q}} = \dfrac{1}{x}^k$, then find the value of k ;

45. Express the following in exponential form.

(i) $\dfrac{625}{1331}$ (ii) 1024   (iii) 1250   (iv) 507   (v) 360

2. Daily Practice

These sets of problems can be used for accelerating the pace of learning

Worksheet 1

1. There were 6416 trees in a forest. In another forest there are three eighth more trees than the first one. Trees in third forest are equal to 550 less than those of all the trees of both the first and second forest put together. Arrange these forests in accord to the increasing number of trees.
2. Find the perimeter of a figure formed by joining three equilateral triangles of side 23.23 cm each.
3. Nithin is 40 m South West of Kavita. Mohini is 430 m South East of Kavita. Mohini is in which direction of Nithin ?

4. Add: $\qquad 16\frac{9}{10} + 106\frac{19}{100} + 21\frac{3}{1000} =$

5. Veena rides her bike to the park for 18 minutes at an average speed of 9 m per second to meet a friend. Veena arrives at the park at 11:00 a.m. and stays there for 58 minutes. Her friend will arrive there at 12:15 p.m. they had a meeting for 32 minutes.

   Try to answer the following questions.

   A. What is the distance between the park and Veena's house?

   B. How long could Veena have to wait for her friend?

   C. How long does Veena stay at the park?

   D. When will Veena leave to go home?

6. Complete the number pattern:

   a. 9, 12, 15, 18, 21, 24, 27, ___, ___, ___

   b. 1, 1,2 , 3, ___, 8 , 13, ______ , ___

   c. 144, 121, 100, _____, _____ , 49, 36, 25, ___ , ___, 4, 1.

   d. $\frac{11}{100}, \frac{12}{110}, \frac{13}{120},$ ______, ______, ______ .

7. $1 + 2 + 3 + \ldots + 100 \qquad = (100 + 1)X\frac{100}{2} = 101\,X\,50 = 5{,}050$

Find the value of $1 + 2 + 3 + ... + 1,000$

8 . Which shape could be one of the faces of a cylinder?

9 . Arrange the following shapes as per their increasing number of faces.

Cylinder, Sphere, Cuboid, Triangular Prism, Rectangular Pyramid.

10 . A train is running at an average speed of 80 km per hour. It is covering up 4 km 4 m more in every interval of 10 minutes than that of a car. Find the average speed of the car.

11 . All the English alphabets are replaced by numbers from 1 to 26. In this way 1 stands for A, 3 for C and so on.

Decode the given message on the basis of above code.

     9   12 15 22 5   13 25 9 14 4 9 1

   ————   ————   ———— ————

12. What least number must be added to 101,090,809 to make the number a multiple of 4?

13. Three angles of a triangle are in such a way that first angle is half of the second and one third of the third. Find all the three angles.

14. The floor of a room a hotel is 12 m long and 10 m wide. 45 tiles of 1 m square were in stock. Tiles come in market in pack of ten tiles. How many more 1m square tiles does the manager need to completely cover the floors of three such rooms?

    I: 15 tiles more than 30 full pack
    II: 5 tiles more than 31 full pack
    III: 25 tiles more than 29 full pack
    IV: 50 tiles more than 25 full pack
    Select your answers

    A: Only I   B: Only II   C: I, II and III   D: Only IV

15 . Mr. Jordon prepares to put fencing around his rectangular kitchen garden of width 95 m and the length 105 m. How long fencing wires does he need?

    A: 190 m   B: 200 m C: 210 m D: 400 m

Worksheet 2

1. A half filled oil container is used to store residue oil of capacity 125 liters. After filling the residue three eighth of the container remained empty. Find the capacity of the container.

2. One tenth of a container is equal to 16 cans of capacity 8 liters each. The entire container can hold ___________ liters of oil.

3. What least number must be subtracted from 219.376 to make the result exactly divisible by 219?   [Ans: 0.157]

4. A train, moving at the speed of 15 m per second, is taking 20 seconds to cross a telephone post. This train can take _______ seconds to cross a 1.5 km long platform.   [Ans : 2 minutes]

5. There are _______ diagonals in a pentagon.

6. A three digit greatest number is divisible by both 3 and 6. This number is also divisible by ________. This number must be an ______________ number.

7. A teacher purchased three types of pens.

   6 boxes of red pens with 40 pens in each box

   5 boxes of blue pens with 20 pens in each box

   Which number is closest to the total pens?

   A: 250   B: 350   C: 400   D: 450

8. All the three digit numbers formed by using digits 4, 3 and 0. If you arrange these numbers in ascending orders then _______a______ comes in the second position and ___b___ comes at last.

9. Mr Jordon prepares to put fencing around his rectangular kitchen garden of width 95 m and the length 105 m. How long fencing wires does he need?

A: 190 m B: 200 m

C: 210 m D: 400 m

10. Half of the half of 98 = ___________ of 196.

11. Sum total of all the numbers formed by using digits 1,3 and 0 only once is ___________.

12. _______ is the only number which is a factor of all the numbers.

13. ________ is the predecessor of smallest six digit odd number.

14. Find the digit present in the thousands place in the product

$(11011 \div 11) \times 7000 = $ _____________

A: 1 B: 11 C: 121 D: 111

15. $\frac{1}{72}$ of a circle is equivalent to ___________

A: 72^0 B: 36^0 C: 5^0 D: 10^0

16. Compare the place value of 3 in 2,309 and 3,283. Find the difference of both the place values of 3. The difference is the _(____) th multiple of 100.

A: 27 B: 30 C: 28 D: 35

17. Write the following in exponential form and radical form.

    a. Cube root of 729

    b. Fifth root of 1990

    c. Square root of 2001

    d. Seventh root of 777

18. Sum total of cube root and square root of a number is equal to 12. Find tenth multiple of that number.

Worksheet 3

1. A regular pentagon has __a___ lines of symmetry less than a hexagon. It
    has _____b _____ lines of symmetry more than an equilateral triangle.
    Both square and equilateral triangle has __ c__ lines of symmetry in all.

	a	b	c
A:	1	2	7
B:	2	4	8
C:	1	2	3
D:	2	4	6

2. Other two angles of a triangle are $2/3^{rd}$ and $1/3^{rd}$ of a right angle
    respectively. Find the measure of all the interior angles of a triangle.

3. Ravi is 3 years older than Mallika but 2 years younger than Kamal. Who is
    youngest among them? Arrange their names in ascending order of their
    age.

4. Total cost of 5 pens and 3 pencils is Rs. 85. Find the total cost of 1 pen
    and 1 pencil if total cost of 3 pens and 2 pencils is Rs. 61.

5. What must be added to make 10982 divisible by 11?

6. Find a factor of 121 which is also a factor of 2020.

7. Complete the following:

a. 321,403,320 =

b. 324,432,543   = ___ X 100,000,000

                              + ____X 10,000,000

                              + ____X 1,000,000

                              + ____X 100,000

                              + ____X 10,000

                              + ____X 1,000

                              + ____X 100

                              + ____X 10

                              + ____X 1

8. Difference of the place value and face value of 8 in 580,554,704 is __.

9. _______ Million = 3,000 thousands.

10. A number greater than the sum total of successor and predecessor of 6 digit greatest number, which is also a multiple of 3 = ________________.

11. _________, 000,000 = ________ million.

12. Complete the expansion in Indo-Arabic Numeration

a. 98,76,54,321 =   90,00,00,000 + 8,00,00,000 + ________ + 6,00,000
+ 50,000 + ________ + 300 + 20 + 1

b. 32,54,03,320 =

c. 32,43,54,576 =

d. 20,30,40,506 =

e. 78,98,70,670 =

13. __________________ is the predecessor of the smallest six digit even number.

14. A greatest 8 digit number divisible by 11 is ____________________.

15. __________________ is the successor of a greatest four digit multiple of 4

16. _______________ is a multiple of 4 which comes after 340890.

17. Find the greatest five digit even number divisible by 8.

18. Write the predecessor of 7 digit greatest number.

19. Calculate the sum total of place values of 3 in the following numbers

20. 34,55,67,505, 30,56,05,506 and 35,05,04,050

21. Difference of the place value and face value of 8 in 65,76,80,653, 78,806 and 48,65,678 = ____________.

22. ____,00,00,000 = 18 crore.

23. Numbers divisible by 2 are also called _________ numbers.

24. _____ is the only even prime number.

25. All prime numbers have only _____ factors. _____ and the number itself.

26. Sum total of 2 eve numbers is always an _______ number.

27. Sum total of an even number and an odd number is always an _____ number.

28. A prime number between 95 and 100 = _________.

29. All the multiples of 8 are also multiples of 2 and ______.

30. All the multiples of _____ and 4 may or may not be a multiple of 8.

31. All the multiples of ___ and _____ are not necessarily multiples of 10.

32. All multiples of 10 are also multiples of _____ and _____.

33. Write in Standard form :

    a.   4,308.3048

    b.   32 hundredth + 121 thousandths

34. If $\frac{2}{5}$ of $40 = \frac{2}{5} X\ 40 = \frac{2X40}{5} = 2X8 = 16$

    c.   What is $\frac{3}{5}$ of 60 ?

35. Add : $\frac{2}{10} + \frac{33}{100} + \frac{121}{1000} + \frac{6}{5}$

36. 19 + 19 tenths + 19 thousandths = __________.

37. $3\frac{1}{2} + 11\frac{7}{8} =$

38. Half of a quarter of 64 = _________________.

39. Multiply : $\frac{10}{121} X\frac{11}{100} X\frac{13}{24} X\frac{11}{26} X\frac{4}{5} =$

40. Tap A can fill up a water tank in 30 minutes and tap B can empty the same water tank in 45 minutes. Tap A will take _____ minutes to fill the tank when both the taps remain open.

Worksheet 4

Complete the following:

a. Exterior angles of a polygon are 1st, 2nd 3rd and 4th multiple of 36^0. Find all the interior angles of this polygon.

[Exterior angle along with corresponding interior angle of any polygon are supplementary to each other.]

b. Interior angles of a triangle are first second and third multiples of 30^0. Find the angles. What is the special name of that triangle?

c. A triangle having _________ right angles is not possible.

d. A triangle having _______ obtuse angles is not possible.

e. Sum total of all the interior angles of a polygon is 540^0. Find the number of sides it has. There are ______ diagonals in this polygon.

f. Sum total of all the interior angles of a polygon is equal to four right angles. It must have at least one ______ angle or at least _______ right angles. They cannot have less than ______ obtuse angles.

g. Identify following triangles:

h. Supplementary angle of complementary angle of 56^0 is equal to

____________________.

i. A quadrilateral having maximum number of ______ right angles is possible.

j. What fraction of right angle is 30^0?

k. A quadrilateral having maximum number of _____ acute angles is possible.

l.   A triangle having two _______ angles or two _______ angles is not possible.

m.   _________ is the smallest three digit even number divisible by 9.

n.   ______ is the set of consecutive prime located in between 1 and 10.

o.   Sum total of the smallest and the greatest four digit numbers formed by without repeating any digits twice is ____________ more than the smallest five digit number.

p.   9,876 + 1,023 = _______________.

      A: 763   B: 899   C: 989   D: 1209

q.   Difference of digits of a two digit number is 7. if digits are reversed then sum total of both the number becomes the predecessor of the three digit smallest number. _________ is the second multiple of this number.

r.   Prime numbers have only two factors ______ and the __________ _______________.

s.   A wall mount clock strikes 2 bells in 2 seconds. This clock will take _______ seconds in striking 10 bells at 10 O'Clock.

t.   Digit 7 will be used for ….. times if we write all the numbers starting from 1 to 200.

u.   If we write five consecutive multiples of five in ascending order then the third value is 100. Find sum total of all the five multiples.

v.   ………… is the least number which must be added to 980 to make the value a square number.

w.   ….., ……………, …………… are three consecutive square numbers just after 100.

x.   Half of a quarter of a number is equal to number P. Again, $P^2 + 2P = 122$. Find the number.

Worksheet 5

1. There are 35,278 students in Class III, 32,184 students in Class IV and 25,375 students in Class V in the schools of a city. Find the total number of students reading in Classes III, IV and V. Among these students 60,324 are girls. Find the number of students who are boys.

2. A person had $ 197,865. He gave $ 50,753 to his wife and $ 75,928 to his son. The rest of the money he gave to his daughter. How much did the daughter get?

3. What should be added to the sum of 3,46,068 and 3,24,263 to get the sum of 8,05,400?

4. There are 4021 students in a school. Each section can accommodate a maximum number of 25 students. There are equal number of students in each section, find their number in each section. Is there any section having less than 25 students? How many such sections are there?

5. Write in standard form:

   32 tens + 54 hundreds + 121 ones = ___________.

6. What must be multiplies to 290,109 to shift 1 from its place to the place occupied by 9?

   A: 10,000   B: 1,000 C: 10   D: 100

7. Sum total of place values of 6 in the following set of numbers = __ .

   26,754,   64,543   23,362

   A: 66,600   B: 66,060 C: 60,606   D: 16,000

8. 4th multiple of the product of all the factors of 101 is _______ more than the 4th multiple of 100.

   A: 2   B: 16   C: 4   D: 40

9. Two third of the half of 123 is the _____ multiple of 41.

   A: 1st B: 2nd C: 3rd D: 4th

10. 776 is the _______________ multiple of 97.

    A: 4th B: 8th C: 5th D: 9th

11. Mohan wants to distribute 129 sweets and 321 almonds amongst his 63 friends equally. Calculate the number of sweets and almonds that remain to Mohan after the distribution.

12. The product of two numbers is 41310. If one of them is 270, find the other.

13. In certain division algorithm the quotient is 57, the divisor is 45 and the remainder is 29, find the dividend.

14. The annual income of Sam is Rs. 98,364. What is his monthly income if he earns an equal amount every month?

15. A number was divided by 97; the quotient was 3806 and the remainder 76. Find the number.

16. When 650 is multiplied by a number, the product is 5590. Find the number.

17. 49,000 fruits were distributed among 1,000 clubs equally. How many fruits did each club get?

18. There are 2,983 boys and 2,175 girls in a school. Find the total enrolment of the school. Find also the number of more boys than girls on the rolls of the school.

19. What should be added to 79,415 to make it the greatest five-digit number?

20. By how much is 89283 is greater than 79382?

21. What should be subtracted from 98989 to get 88888?

22. There are ____ vertices, ____ faces and ______ edges in a cuboid.

23. Two cubical block of edge 30 cm each joined side by side to form a cuboidal block. Find the surface area of the top and bottom part of that cuboid.

24. Malavika prepared a 25 m long rope by joining different segments of 200 cm each. Find the number of segments she used for making that rope.

25. ______ is the predecessor of smallest four digit multiple of 6.

26. Which of the following is greater between each of the two numbers?
    (a) 3^{30} and 7^{15}　　　(b) 2^{25} and 4^{14}　　　(c) 2^{21} and 3^{14}

27. If $7^n = 2401$, then $7^{n-5} =$ ________.

28. If $(a^{b^c}) = 6561$, then find the least possible value of (a.b.c), where a, b, and c are integers.

29. If $5^{n-3} = 625$, then 5^{n+3} is ______.

30. What fraction of all the numbers located in between 1 and 200 are square numbers?

31. One fifth of one seventh of 35,070 = ………………

32. Answer the following:

Q 1.   If a, b, c are distinct real numbers, find the number of real solutions to

$$\frac{(x-a)(x-b)}{(c-a)(c-b)} + \frac{(x-b)(x-c)}{(a-b)(a-c)} + \frac{(x-c)(x-a)}{(b-c)(b-a)} + 1 = 0.$$

Q 2.   Find the real roots of the equation

$$x^2 + 2ax + \frac{1}{16} = -a + \sqrt{a^2 + x - \frac{1}{16}}$$

where $0 < a < \dfrac{1}{4}$.

Q 3.   Solve:

$$\sqrt{x + 14 - 8\sqrt{x-2}} + \sqrt{x + 23 - 10\sqrt{x-2}} = 3.$$

Q 4.   Find out the area of the triangle whose sides are 8, 17, 15.

Q 5.   If $a = (\sqrt{3} + \sqrt{2})^{-3}$ and $b = (\sqrt{3} - \sqrt{2})^{-3}$, find the value of $(a+1)^{-1} + (b+1)^{-1}$

Q 6.   If a, b, c are positive integers such that

$$\frac{a}{3} = \frac{b}{4} = \frac{c}{5} \quad \text{and} \quad abc = 1620,$$

find the value of b.

3. Junior Scientist Exam

Set 1

1. The city of Madras has a population of 25 lakhs. If each citizen of Madras has an asset of value not more than 2 lakhs, show that two of the citizens have assets of the same value, when corrected to the nearest integer.

2. Given 10 triangles show that two of them are *either* equilateral *or* isosceles but not equilateral *or* acute angled but not isosceles *or* obtuse angled but not isosceles *or* right angled but not isosceles.

3. A is a subset of the arithmetic progression $2, 7, 12, \cdots, 152$ having 16 elements. Show that there are two distinct elements of A whose sum is 159. What can you say if A has 14 elements?

4. Given three points in the interior of a right angled triangle, show that two of them are at a distance not greater than the maximum of the lengths of the sides containing the right angle.

5. If a line is coloured with 11 colours show that there exist two points whose distance apart is an integer which have the same colour.

6. Show that in any set of ten distinct two digit numbers there exists two subsets which have the same sum.

Set 2

Write in simplest form:

#			#		
1.	$5^2 \cdot 5^3 =$		23.	$7^3 \cdot 7^2 =$	
2.	$5^2 \cdot 5^4 =$		24.	$7^2 \cdot 7^3 =$	
3.	$5^2 \cdot 5^5 =$		25.	$(-4)^3 \cdot (-4)^{11} =$	
4.	$2^7 \cdot 2^1 =$		26.	$(-4)^{11} \cdot (-4)^3 =$	
5.	$2^8 \cdot 2^1 =$		27.	$(0.2)^3 \cdot (0.2)^{11} =$	
6.	$2^9 \cdot 2^1 =$		28.	$(0.2)^{11} \cdot (0.2)^3 =$	
7.	$3^6 \cdot 3^2 =$		29.	$(-2)^9 \cdot (-2)^5 =$	
8.	$3^6 \cdot 3^3 =$		30.	$(-2.7)^5 \cdot (-2.7)^9 =$	
9.	$3^6 \cdot 3^4 =$		31.	$3.1^6 \cdot 3.1^6 =$	
10.	$7^{15} \cdot 7 =$		32.	$57^6 \cdot 57^6 =$	
11.	$7^{16} \cdot 7 =$		33.	$z^6 \cdot z^6 =$	
12.	$11^{12} \cdot 11^2 =$		34.	$4 \cdot 2^9 =$	
13.	$11^{12} \cdot 11^4 =$		35.	$4^2 \cdot 2^9 =$	
14.	$11^{12} \cdot 11^6 =$		36.	$16 \cdot 2^9 =$	
15.	$23^5 \cdot 23^2 =$		37.	$16 \cdot 4^3 =$	
16.	$23^6 \cdot 23^3 =$		38.	$9 \cdot 3^5 =$	
17.	$23^7 \cdot 23^4 =$		39.	$3^5 \cdot 9 =$	
18.	$13^7 \cdot 13^3 =$		40.	$3^5 \cdot 27 =$	
19.	$15^7 \cdot 15^3 =$		41.	$5^7 \cdot 25 =$	
20.	$17^7 \cdot 17^3 =$		42.	$5^7 \cdot 125 =$	
21.	$x^7 \cdot x^3 =$		43.	$2^{11} \cdot 4 =$	
22.	$y^7 \cdot y^3 =$		44.	$2^{11} \cdot 16 =$	

45. Simplify: $(1 + 2 + 3 + \dots 1{,}000) - (2 + 4 + 6 + \dots + 2{,}000)$

46. A number is equal to four digit number which is also a cube number. After subtracting 1 from that number it becomes a three digit greatest number. Find the number.

47. What least number can be subtracted from the greatest seven digit number to make the value divisible by 8?

***.

4. Combined Worksheets

Worksheet 1

If $a^2 - \sqrt{3}a + 1 = 0$, what is the value of $a^3 + \dfrac{1}{a^3}$?

Solution : Given that $\quad a^2 - \sqrt{3}a + 1 = 0$

$$\text{or, } a^2 + 1 = \sqrt{3}a \qquad \text{or, } \frac{a^2+1}{a} = \sqrt{3}$$

$$\text{or, } \frac{a^2}{a} + \frac{1}{a} = \sqrt{3} \qquad \text{or, } a + \frac{1}{a} = \sqrt{3}$$

Given expression $= a^3 + \dfrac{1}{a^3}$

$$= \left(a + \frac{1}{a}\right)^3 - 3a \cdot \frac{1}{a}\left(a + \frac{1}{a}\right)$$

$$= \left(\sqrt{3}\right) - 3\left(\sqrt{3}\right) \quad [\because a + \frac{1}{a} = \sqrt{3}]$$

$$= 3\sqrt{3} - 3\sqrt{3}$$

$$= 0$$

1. Find the cube with the help of the formulae :
   (a) $2x + 5$ (b) $2x^2 + 3y^2$ (c) $4a - 5x^2$ (d) $7m^2 - 2n$ (e) 403 (f) 998
   (g) $2a - b - 3c$ (h) $2x + 3y + z$

2. Simplify :
   (a) $(4a - 3b)^3 - 3(4a - 3b)^2(2a - 3b) + 3(4a - 3b)(2a - 3b)^2 - (2a - 3b)^3$
   (b) $(2x + y)^3 + 3(2x + y)^2(2x - y) + 3(2x + y)(2x - y)^2 + (2x - y)^3$
   (c) $(7x + 3b)^3 - (5x + 3b)^3 - 6x(7x + 3b)(5x + 3b)$
   (d) $(x - 15)^3 + (16 - x)^3 + 3(x - 15)(16 - x)$
   (e) $(a + b + c)^3 - (a - b - c)^3 - 6(b + c)\{a^2 - (b + c)^2\}$
   (f) $(m + n)^6 - (m - n)^6 - 12mn(m^2 - n^2)^2$
   (g) $(x + y)(x^2 - xy + y^2) + (y + z)(y^2 - yz + z^2) + (z + x)(z^2 - zx + x^2)$
   (h) $(2x + 3y - 4z)^3 + (2x - 3y + 4z)^3 + 12x\{4x^2 - (3y - 4z)^2\}$

3. If $a - b = 5$ and $ab = 36$, what is the value of $a^3 - b^3$?

4. If $a^3 - b^3 = 513$ and $a - b = 3$, what is the value of ab ?

5. If $x = 19$ and $y = -12$, find the value of $8x^3 + 36x^2y + 54xy^2 + 27y^3$.

6. If $a = 15$, what is the value of $8a^3 + 60a^2 + 150a + 130$?

7. Sum total of five consecutive integers exceeds the fifth multiple of smallest four digit number by eighteen. Find product of smallest and greatest number of the series.

8. If $a+b=m$, $a^2+b^2=n$ and $a^3+b^3=p^3$, show that, $m^3+2p^3=3mn$.

9. If $x+y=1$, show that, $x^3+y^3-xy=(x-y)^2$

10. If $a+b=3$ and $ab=2$, find the value of (a) a^2-ab+b^2 and (b) a^3+b^3.

11. If $a-b=5$ and $ab=36$, find the value of (a) a^2+ab+b^2 and (b) a^3-b^3.

12. If $m+\dfrac{1}{m}=a$, find the value of $m^3+\dfrac{1}{m^3}$.

13. If $x-\dfrac{1}{x}=p$, find the value of $x^3-\dfrac{1}{x^3}$.

14. If $a-\dfrac{1}{a}=1$, show that, $a^3-\dfrac{1}{a^3}=4$.

15. If $a+b+c=0$, show that,

  (a) $a^3+b^3+c^3=3abc$ (b) $\dfrac{(b+c)^2}{3bc}+\dfrac{(c+a)^2}{3ca}+\dfrac{(a+b)^2}{3ab}=1$.

16. If $p-q=r$, show that, $p^3-q^3-r^3=3pqr$

17. If $2x-\dfrac{2}{x}=3$, show that, $8\left(x^3-\dfrac{1}{x^3}\right)=63$.

18. If $a=\sqrt{6}+\sqrt{5}$, find the value of $\dfrac{a^6-1}{a^3}$.

19. Find value of the following.

A: $(1+2+3\ldots+1,000)+(1+2+3+\ldots+500)=$ ....

B: $\left(1+\dfrac{1}{2}\right)\left(1+\dfrac{1}{3}\right)\ldots\left(1+\dfrac{1}{1000}\right)=$ ....

C: $(1+2+3+\ldots+5.000)=$ ....

D: A X A X A = 1331; Find the value of A^2+2A+1

20. Half of a number A exceeds quarter of another number B by 25. Find the value of $(4A^2+B^2)$.

21. It is observed that after adding 1 to a number it becomes square of the smallest three digit number. Find the value of fifth multiple of that number.

22. What must be added to the greatest six digit even number to make the value a square number?

23. A number series is as follows: 1, 1, 2, 3, 5...... If this series continues then find the sum total of tenth and eleventh number.

24. Half of a number is equal to sum total of two consecutive square numbers. Find sum total of fifth and tenth multiple of that number.

Worksheet 2

Factorise

1. $a^2 + ab + ac + bc$
2. $ab + a - b - 1$
3. $(x-y)(x+y) + (x-y)(y+z) + (x-y)(z+x)$
4. $ab(x-y) - bc(x-y)$
5. $9x^2 + 24x + 16$
6. $a^4 - 27a^2 + 1$
7. $x^4 - 6x^2y^2 + y^4$
8. $(a^2 - b^2)(x^2 - y^2) + 4abxy$
9. $4a^2 - 12ab + 9b^2 - 4c^2$
10. $9x^4 - 45a^2x^2 + 36a^4$
11. $a^2 + 6a + 8 - y^2 + 2y$
12. $16x^2 - 25y^2 - 8xz + 10yz$
13. $2b^2c^2 + 2c^2a^2 + 2a^2b^2 - a^4 - b^4 - c^4$
14. $x^2 + 13x + 36$
15. $x^4 + x^2 - 20$
16. $a^2 - 30a + 216$
17. $x^6y^6 - x^3y^3 - 6$
18. $a^8 - a^4 - 2$
19. $a^2b^2 - 8ab - 105$
20. $x^2 - 37a - 650$
21. $4x^4 - 25x^2 + 36$
22. $12x^2 - 38x + 20$
23. $9x^2y^2 - 5xy^2 - 14y^2$
24. $4x^4 - 27x^2 - 81$
25. $ax^2 + (a^2 + 1)x + a$
26. $3(a^2 + 2a)^2 - 22(a^2 + 2a) + 40$
27. $14(x+z)^2 - 29(x+z)(x+1) - 15(x+1)^2$
28. $(4a - 3b)^2 - 2(4a - 3b)(a + 2b) - 35(a + 2b)^2$
29. $(a-1)x^2 + a^2xy + (a+1)y^2$
30. $24x^4 - 3x$
31. $(a^2 + b^2)^3 + 8a^3b^3$
32. $x^3 + 3x^2 + 3x + 2$
33. $a^3 - 6a^2 + 12a - 9$
34. $a^3 - 9b^3 + (a+b)^3$
35. $8x^3 + 12x^2 + 6x - 63$
36. $8a^3 + \dfrac{b^3}{27}$
37. $a^3 - \dfrac{1}{8}$
38. $\dfrac{a^6}{27} - b^6$
39. $4a^2 + \dfrac{1}{4a^2} - 2 + 4a - \dfrac{1}{a}$
40. $(3a + 1)^3 - (2a = 3)^3$
41. $(x+5)(x-9) - 15$
42. $(x+2)(x+3)(x+4)(x+5) - 48$

43. Product of four consecutive numbers is equal to 24×10^8. Find sum total of first and fourth numbers.

44. Sum total of a number and its reciprocal is equal to 20.05. Find the number.

Worksheet 3

Q1 A wooden bookshelf has external dimensions as follows:
Height = 110 cm , Depth = 25 cm , and Breadth = 85 cm (see figure). The
thickness of the plank is 5 cm everywhere. The external faces are to be
polished and the inner faces are to be painted. If the rate of polishing is 20
paise per cm^2 and the rate of painting is 10 paise per cm^2, find the total
expenses required for polishing and painting the surface of the bookshelf.

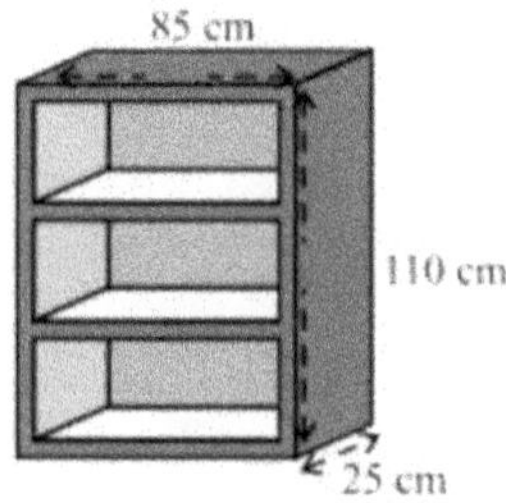

2. The diagram shows the net of a right cylinder. Find the volume of the
cylinder, in cm^3

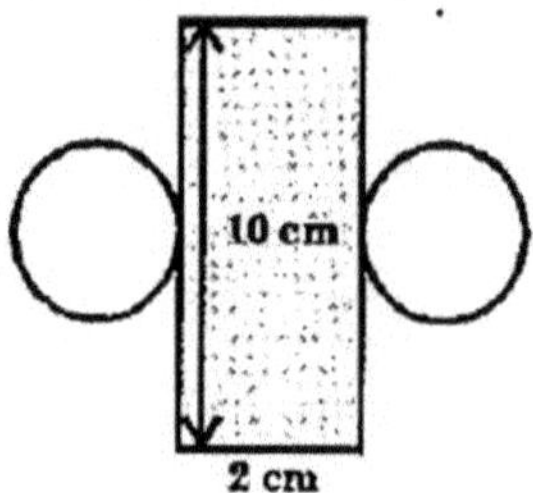

3. A rectangle and a square are attached side by side to form a definite pattern. Side of
square is equal to breadth of the rectangle. Length is four times longer than the
breadth. Find area of entire figure in the form of multiple of that breadth.

4. Half of a rectangle is equal to quarter of a square of side 40 cm in terms of their area.
Find the total outer boundary of that shape if both the sides kept side by side.

5. Area of three squares of side 1 m 1 cm each is equal to a rectangle of breadth 202 cm.
Find length of that rectangle.

6. Find area of four walls of a room of dimension 8 m X 6 m X 5 m. Also find the cost of white washing of that room at the rate of Rs 100 per square m.

07. Length of the fence of a trapezium shaped field ABCD is 120 m. If BC = 48 m, CD = 17 m and AD = 40 m, find the area of this field. Side AB is perpendicular to the parallel sides AD and BC.

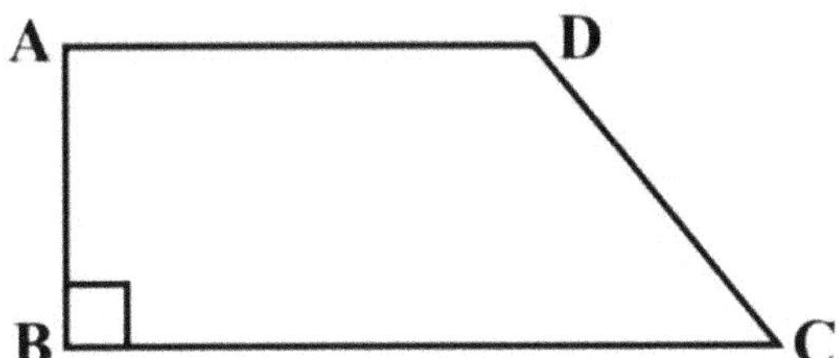

08. Volume of a cube is 3375 cm^3. Find total surface area of that cube. Also find the cost of painting that cube at the rate of Rs 10 per cm^2.

09. An open box of length 1.5m, breadth 1m, and height 1m is to be made for use on a trolley for carrying garden waste. How much sheet metal will be required to make this box? The inside and outside surface of the box is to be painted with rust proof paint. At a rate of 150 rupees per sqm, how much will it cost to paint the box?

10. the perimeter of a trapezium is 104m,its non-parallel sides are 18m and 22m, and its altitude is 16m.find the area of trapezium

11. Complete the following table:

Shape	Side (cm)	Volume (cu.cm.)	Surface Area (sq. cm.)
Cube	10		
Cube		1331	
Cube			2400
Cube			
Cube			

12. Total surface area of a cube is 5,400 cm^2. Find volume of that cube.

13. Diagram of the adjacent picture frame has outer dimensions = 24cm ×28 cm and inner dimensions 16cm ×20cm. Find the area of each section of the frame, if the width of each section is same.

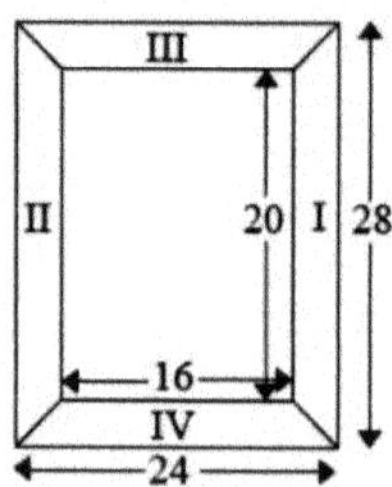

14. Complete the following: ...

Total Surface Area (TSA) of a Cylinder

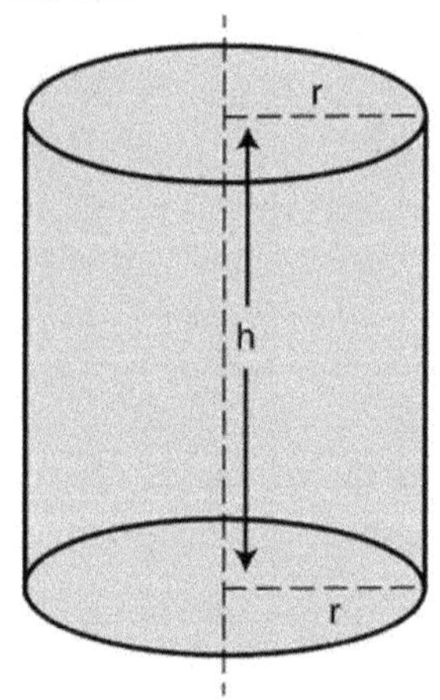

Formula:

TSA = 2πr(r + h)

here,

$\pi = \dfrac{22}{7} = 3.141$,

r = radius, h = height

Radius (r) in cm	Height (h) in cm	Volume (v)
21 cm	15 cm	....
7 cm	28 cm	....
14 cm	58 cm	....

15. Total surface area of a cube is 600 cm^3. Find its volume.

Worksheet 4

01. The area of a trapezium is 475cm^2 and the height is 19 cm, then the lengths of smaller side of two parallel sides if one side is 4 cm greater than the other is

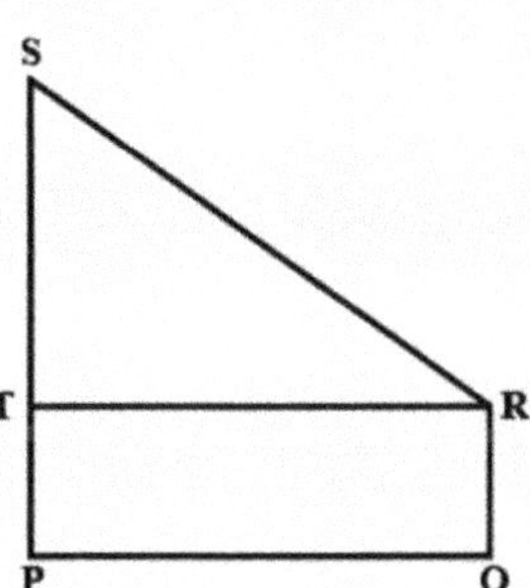

02. **Assertion**

Total surface area of the cylinder having radius of the base 14 cm and height 30 cm is 3872 cm^2.

Reason

If r be the radius and h be the height of the cylinder, then total surface area $= (2\pi rh + 2\pi r^2)$

    A   Both Assertion and Reason are correct and Reason is the correct explanation for Assertion

    B   Both Assertion and Reason are correct but Reason is not the correct explanation for Assertion

    C   Assertion is correct but Reason is incorrect

3. Dimension of a ply board is 1 m X 30 cm X 2.5 cm. Find its volume. Also find total cost of painting this board at the rate of Rs 3 per cm^2.

04. A road roller takes 750 complete revolutions to move once over to level a road. Find the area of the road if the diameter of a road roller is 84 cm and lenght is 1 m.

05. A tent is in the form of a right circular cylinder, surmounted by a cone. The diameter of the cylinder is 24 m. The height of the cylindrical portion is 11 m, while the vertex of the cone is 16 m above the ground.The curved surface area of the cylindrical portion is

   A $(246\pi)\text{m}^2$

   B $(264\pi)\text{m}^2$

   C $(426\pi)\text{m}^2$

6. Mr Ravikumar observed that Cistern A can fill up a water tank in 45 minutes, Cistern B in 1 hour and cistern C in 1 hour 15 minutes. If all the three cisterns kept open then two such water tanks will be filled up in …… h …… minutes

7. Monika can finish her project works in 8 days, Snehal can finish similar project work in 12 days. Both of them jointly can finish the project work in ….. days.

8. one third of three seventeenth of 51,102 = …………………………

***

5. Mensuration

I: Calculate the outer boundary of the following polygons.

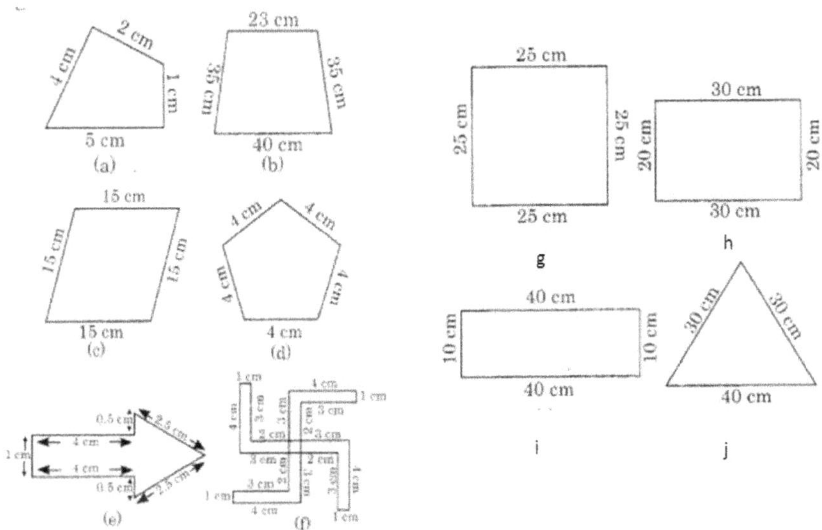

II: Outer boundary of a rectangle is two times that of a square of side 64 cm. If ratio of the length and breadth of that rectangle is 5:3 then find area of that rectangle.

III: Solve the following.

1. A closed cylindrical tank, made of thin iron-sheet, has diameter 8.4 m and height 5.4 m. How much metal sheet to the nearest m^2 is used in making this tank, if $\dfrac{1}{15}$ of the sheet actually used was wasted in making the tank ?

2. A building has 8 right cylindrical pillars whose cross sectional diameter is 1 m and whose height is 4.2 m. Find the expenditure to paint these pillars at the rate of Rs.24 per m^2

Important rules …

Sl. No	Name	Figure	Lateral or Curved Surface Area (sq.units)	Total Surface Area (sq.units)	Volume (cu.units)
1	Right circular cylinder		$2\pi rh$	$2\pi r(h + r)$	$\pi r^2 h$
2	Right circular hollow cylinder		$2\pi h(R + r)$	$2\pi(R + r)(R - r + h)$	$\pi R^2 h - \pi r^2 h$ $\pi h(R^2 - r^2)$ $\pi h(R + r)(R - r)$
3	Right circular cone		πrl	$\pi r(l + r)$	$\dfrac{1}{3}\pi r^2 h$
4	Frustum		- - - - - - -	- - - - - - - - - - - - -	$\dfrac{1}{3}\pi h(R^2 + r^2 + Rr)$
5	Sphere		$4\pi r^2$	- - -	$\dfrac{4}{3}\pi r^3$
6	Hollow sphere		- - -	- - -	$\dfrac{4}{3}\pi(R^3 - r^3)$
7	Hemisphere		$2\pi r^2$	$3\pi r^2$	$\dfrac{2}{3}\pi r^3$
8	Hollow Hemisphere		$2\pi(R^2 + r^2)$	$2\pi(R^2 + r^2) + \pi(R^2 - r^2)$	$\dfrac{2}{3}\pi(R^3 - r^3)$

9	Cone			

9. Cone

$l = \sqrt{h^2 + r^2}$

$h = \sqrt{l^2 - r^2}$

$r = \sqrt{l^2 - h^2}$

CSA of a cone = Area of the sector

$\pi rl \quad = \dfrac{\theta}{360} \times \pi r^2$

Length of the sector = Base circumference of the cone

10. Volume of water flows out through a pipe

= {Cross section area × Speed × Time }

11. No. of new solids obtained by recasting

$= \dfrac{\text{Volume of the solid which is melted}}{\text{volume of one solid which is made}}$

12	Conversions	1 m³ = 1000 litres , 1 d.m³ = 1 litre . 1000 cm³ = 1 litre . 1000 litres = 1 kl

***.

***.

6. Self Practice

Worksheet 1

1: An inheritance of $ 24,000 is to be divided among three trusts, with the second trust receiving twice as moch as the first tru st. The three trusts pay interest annually at the rales of 9%, 10%. and 6%, respectively; and return a total in interest of $ 2210 at the end of the first year. How much was invested in each trust?

2: An oil refinery produces low sulfur and high sulfur fuel Each ton of low-sulfur fuel requires 5 minutes in the blending plant and 4 minules in the refining plant: each ton of high sulfur fuel require; 4 minutes in the blending plant and 2 minutes in the refining planl. If the blend- 109 plant is available for 3 hours and lhe refining plant is available for 2 hours. How many tons of each lype of fuel should be manufactured so that the plants are fully used?

3: A plastics manufacturer makes two types of plastic: regular and special. Each ton of regular plastic requires 2 hours in plant A and 5 hours in planl B each ton of special plastic requires 2 hours In plant A and 3 hours in piant B. Jf plant A is available 11 hours per day and plant B is available 15 hours per day, how many tons of each type of plastic can be made daily so thm the plants are fully used?

4: A dietician is preparing a meal consisting of foods A, B and C. Each ounce of food A contains 2 units of protein, 3 units of fat and 4 units of carbohydrate. Each ounce of food B contains 3 units of protein, 2 units of fat and 1 unit of carbohydrate. Each ounce of food C contains 3 units of protein, 3 units of fat and 2 units of carbohydrate. If the meal must provide exactly 25 units of protein, 24 units of fat and 21 units of carbohydrate how many ounces of each type of food should be used?

5: How many times do 6 occur if we write all the natural numbers from 1 to 200?

6: Simplify:

a. $\dfrac{x^4 - 3x^3 + 2x^2 + 3x - 1}{x^2 + 2x - 1}$

d. $\dfrac{x^4 + 3x^3 + 5x^2 + 12x + 4}{x^2 + 3x + 1}$

b. $\dfrac{x^4 + 2x^3 + 2x^2 + 4x + 1}{x^2 + 2}$

e. $\dfrac{x^6 + 3x^5 + x^4 + x^2 + 3}{x^4 + 1}$

c. $\dfrac{x^4 + x^3 - 2x^2 + 14x + 1}{x^2 - 4}$

f. $\dfrac{x^6 - 1}{x^5 - 1}$

g. $300abc + 420xyz$

j. $36x^{-3}y^4 + 20x^{-5}y^2$

k. $125x^{-3}y^{-4} + 500x^{-5}y^{-2}$

h. $121x^4 - 165z$

i. $24x^2y^3 - 48x^3y^2$

l. $x(3x-1)^2 + 2x^2(3x-1)$

7: A wall mount clock strikes three belles at 3 O'Clock in 3 seconds. Find the time taken by this clock to strike 11 bells at 11 O'Clock.

8: The shape of a garden is rectangular in the middle and semicircular at the ends. Find the area and the perimeter of this garden. [Length of rectangle is 20 − (3.5 + 3.5) metres]

9: A flooring tile has the shape of a parallelogram whose base is 24 cm and the corresponding height is 10 cm. How many such tiles are required to cover a floor of area 1080 m²? (If required you can split the tiles in whatever way you want to fill up the corners).

10: An ant is moving around a few food pieces of different shapes scattered on the floor. For which food-piece would the ant have to take a longer round? Remember, the circumference of a circle can be obtained by using the expression C = 2πr, where r is the radius of the circle.

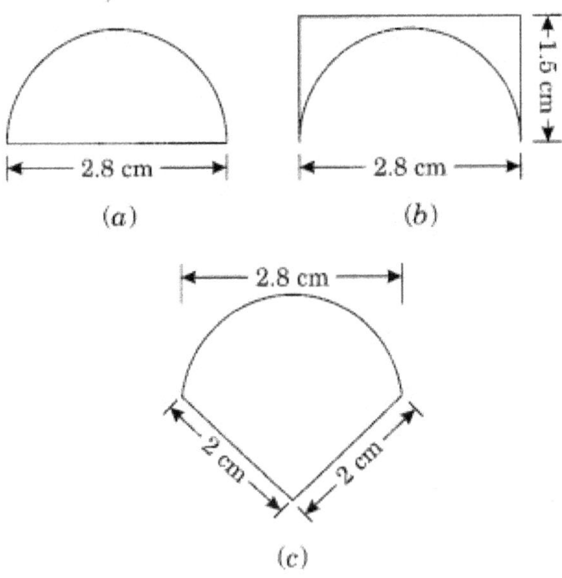

11: Find the common factors of the given terms.
(i) 12x, 36
(ii) 2y, 22xy
(iii) 14pq, $28p^2q^2$
(iv) 2x, $3x^2$, 4
(v) 6abc, $24ab^2$, $12a^2b$
(vi) $16x^3$, $-4x^2$, 32x
(vii) 10pq, 20qr, 30rp
(viii) $3x^2y^3$, $10x^3y^2$, $6x^2y^2z$
(ix) xy^2z^3, $x^3y^4z^2$, $x^9y^4z^3$
(x) 121 x^2, 1331 x^3, 11 x
(xi) 169 a^2b^4, 13 ab^2
(xii) 100 m^3n^6, 1000 m^6n^9

12: Factorise the following expressions.

(i) $7x - 42$

(ii) $6p - 12q$

(iii) $7a^2 + 14a$

(iv) $-16z + 20z^3$

(v) $20l^2m + 30alm$

(vi) $5x^2y - 15xy^2$

(vii) $10a^2 - 15b^2 + 20c^2$

(viii) $-4a^2 + 4ab - 4ca$

(ix) $x^2yz + xy^2z + xyz^2$

(x) $ax^2y + bxy^2 + cxyz$

(xi) $x^2 + xy + 8x + 8y$

(xii) $15xy - 6x + 5y - 2$

(xiii) $ax + bx - ay - by$

(xiv) $15pq + 15 + 9q + 25p$

(xv) $z - 7 + 7xy - xyz$

(xv) $121a^2 + 44a + 4$

13: Cistern A can fill up a water tank in 45 minutes and Cistern B can fill up the same water tank in 1 hr 30 minutes. If both the cisterns kept open then they will jointly fill up the water tank in …………… minutes.

14: A football team won 10 matches out of the total number of matches they played. If their win percentage was 40, then how many matches did they play in all?

15: If Chameli had ₹ 600 left after spending 75% of her money, how much did she have in the beginning?

16: If 60% of people in a city like a cricket, 30% like football and the remaining like other games, then what per cent of the people like other games? If the total number of people are 50 lakh, find the exact number who like each type of game.

17: Cinthelenia saved Rs 700 after spending 90% of her monthly income. She donated 2% of her annual income. Find the amount donated by her.

18: Find the ratio of the following:

(a) speed of a cycle 15 km per hour to the speed of scooter 30 km per hour.

(b) 5 m to 10 km

(c) 50 paise to ₹ 5

19: 20% of 60% of $1/12^{th}$ of 600,600 = …………………………………..

20: Half of a quarter of 800,800 = ……………………….

Combined Evaluation

1. A radar device has an antenna that revolves at a constant rate. The graph shows the number of revolutions the device will make over time.

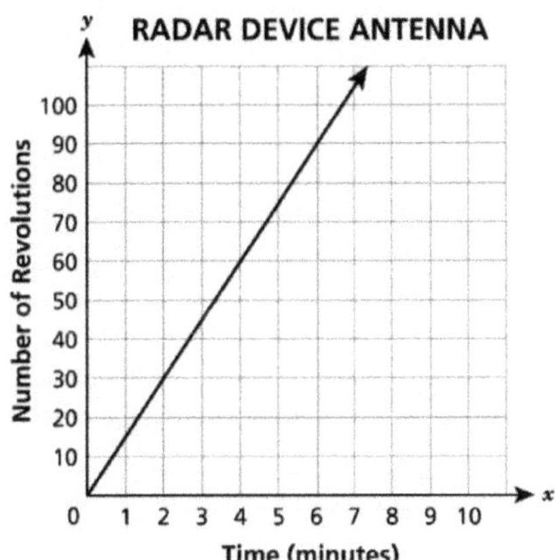

Which table shows the data for an antenna that revolves at exactly twice the rate of the antenna described in the graph?

A

Time (minutes)	Number of Revolutions
15	315
30	660

C

Time (minutes)	Number of Revolutions
20	40
25	50

B

Time (minutes)	Number of Revolutions
18	450
36	900

D

Time (minutes)	Number of Revolutions
22	660
24	720

2: Cistern A fills up an empty water tank in 1.5 hours and cistern B can fill it up in 1 hour. Calculate the time taken by both the cisterns to fill up 3 such water tanks.

3. A fish tank is in the form of a cuboid, external measures of that cuboid are 80 cm ×40 cm ×30 cm. The base, side faces and back face are to be covered with a coloured paper. Find the area of the paper needed in cm^2

4. The dimensions of a Cinema Hall are 100 m, 60 m and 15 m. How many person can sit in the hall, if each requires 150 m^3 of air ?

5. A cylindrical container with internal radius of its base 10 cm, contains water up to a height of 7 cm. Find the area of the wet surface of the cylinder.

6. The octagon shown below has eight congruent sides. The given measures of the octagon are rounded to the nearest tenth of a centimeter.

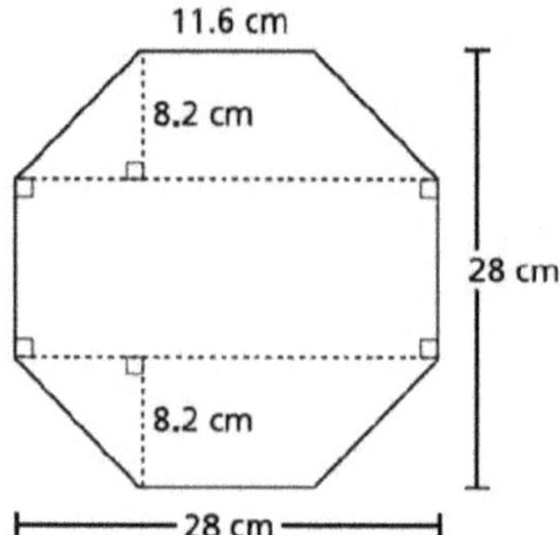

What is the area, to the nearest square centimeter, of the octagon?

7. A cubical box of dimension 12 cm X 50 cm X 90 cm is filled with water. 10% of this box is empty. Find possible dimensions of the empty portion of this box.

8. Find the value of x if x = a 3 + a 2 + a + a -1 a -2 + 11; and a = $\dfrac{\sqrt[3]{0.003125}}{\sqrt[3]{0.064}}$.

9. $x + \dfrac{1}{x} = 2$; Find the value of P if P $= x^{100} + x^{100} + \ldots + x^1$

10. Product of two consecutive positive integer is equal to 10100. Find the numbers.

11. A set of data is represented on the scatter plot below.

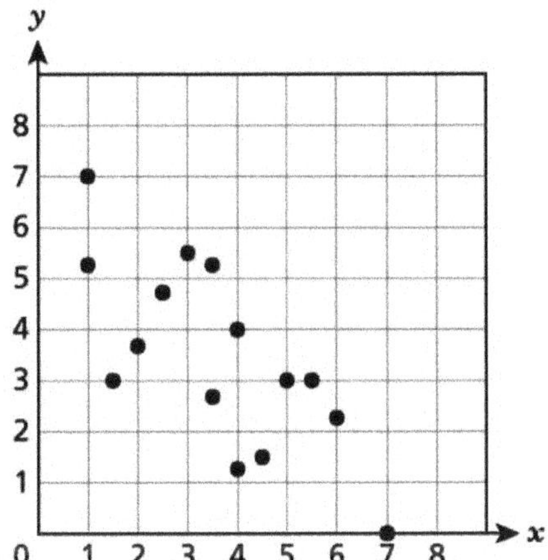

Which equation **best** models the set of data?

A $y = -\dfrac{3}{4}x + 6$

C $y = -6x + \dfrac{3}{4}$

B $y = \dfrac{3}{4}x - 6$

D $y = 6x - \dfrac{3}{4}$

12. A fish tank is in the form of a cuboid, external measures of that cuboid are 80 cm ×40 cm ×30 cm. The base, side faces and back face are to be covered with a coloured paper. Find the area of the paper needed in cm^2

13. The dimensions of a Cinema Hall are 100 m, 60 m and 15 m. How many person can sit in the hall, if each requires 150 m^3 of air ?

14. A cylindrical container with internal radius of its base 10 cm, contains water up to a height of 7 cm. Find the area of the wet surface of the cylinder.

15. A building has 8 right cylindrical pillars whose cross sectional diameter is 1 m and whose height is 4.2 m. Find the expenditure to paint these pillars at the rate of Rs.24 per m^2

16. Calculate the temperature at which reading of Fahrenheit scale will be twice that of Celsius scale.

17. On the coordinate plane below, rectangle ABCD is rotated 90° clockwise about the origin to form rectangle WXYZ.

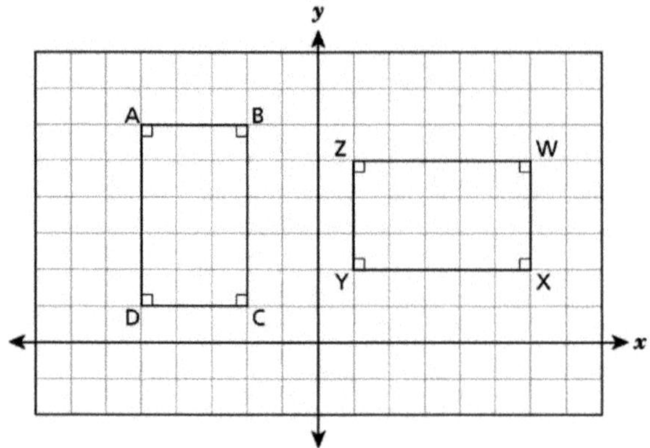

Which statement about the relationship between rectangle ABCD and rectangle WXYZ is true?

A $\overline{DA} \cong \overline{YZ}$

C $\overline{BC} \cong \overline{YZ}$

B $\overline{DC} \cong \overline{XY}$

D $\overline{AB} \cong \overline{WX}$

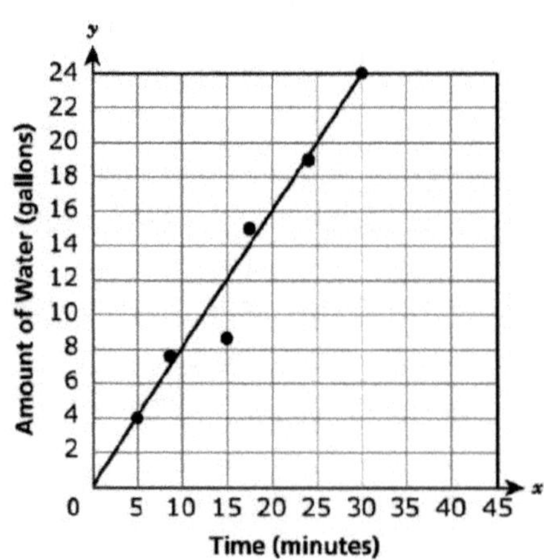

18. If the rate, in gallons per minute, continues, approximately how many gallons of water will flow from the hose in 45 minutes?

19. What fraction of all the numbers starting from 1 to 1010 are multiples of 101?

20. Sum total of a natural number and its reciprocal is equal to 20.05.

21. $\sqrt[2]{(x + x^2 + x^3 + x^4 + x^5 + x^6 + \cdots x^{100}) \times \frac{101}{50}} = P;$

Find the value of P if x = 1001^0.

22. Functions W and Z are both linear functions of x.

Function W

$$y = -\frac{1}{16}x + 30$$

Function Z

x	0	1	2	3
y	15.8	15.76	15.72	15.68

Which statement comparing the functions is true?

A   The slope of Function W is equal to the slope of Function Z.

B   The slope of Function W is less than the slope of Function Z.

C   The y-intercept of Function W is equal to the y-intercept of Function Z.

D   The y-intercept of Function W is less than the y-intercept of Function Z.

23. Triangle BCD is rotated $180°$ clockwise and then dilated by a factor of 4 centered at the origin. The resulting image is triangle $B'C'D'$. Which statement about the two triangles is true?

A   The area of $\triangle BCD$ is 4 times the area of $\triangle B'C'D'$.

B   The perimeter of $\triangle BCD$ is 4 times the perimeter of $\triangle B'C'D'$.

C   The corresponding sides of $\triangle BCD$ and $\triangle B'C'D'$ are congruent.

D   The corresponding angles of $\triangle BCD$ and $\triangle B'C'D'$ are congruent.

24. At a local basketball game, all tickets are the same price and all souvenirs are the same price. Mr. Smith bought 2 tickets to this basketball game and 1 souvenir for a total of $17.25. Ms. Lockhart bought 5 tickets to the same game and 2 souvenirs for a total of $42.00. How much was a ticket to this game?

25. Half of a natural number x and quarter of its reciprocal is equal to 4. 03125. Find the value of $3\sqrt[3]{x} + 5\sqrt{x} + \frac{x}{10} + \sqrt[3]{x}\frac{3}{100}$.

26. Three wall bells toll at an interval of 20 seconds, 5 minutes and 12 minutes respectively. 11:30 A.M. was the first interval during which all the three bells toll together. Find the second interval after which all these three bells toll together.

27. The radius of the base of a right circular cylinder is 3 cm and height is 7 cm. Find the curved surface area (in sq. cm.)

28. A cylinder has a diameter of 20 cm. The area of the curved surface is 100 cm^2 (sq. cm). The height of the cylinder correct to one decimal place is 1.6 cm

29. The dimensions of a car petrol tank are 50 cm $\times$ 32 cm $\times$ 24 cm, which is full of petrol. If car's average consumption is 15 km per litre, find the maximum distance that can be covered by the car.

30. Which function of x has the **least** value for the y-intercept?

   A $y = -4x + 15$ C $y = 2x - 3$

   B 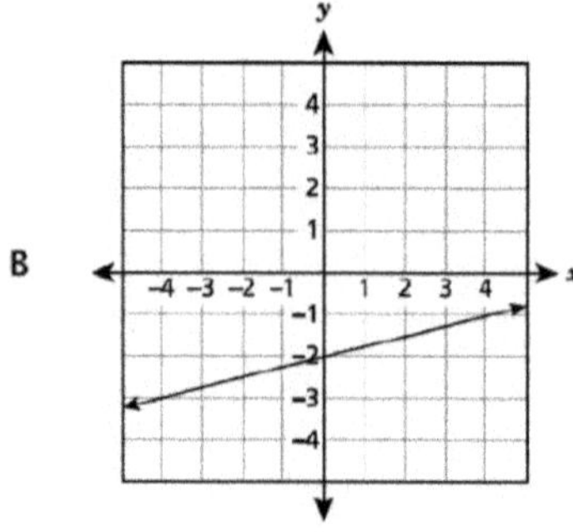   D 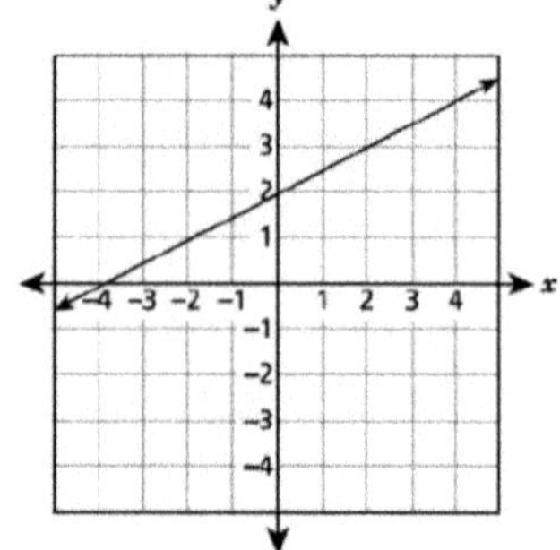

31. Factorize each of the following expressions:

(i) $x^2 + 6x + 8$ (ii) $x^2 + 4x - 21$ (iii) $x^3 - 8 - x + 2$

(iv) $x^2 - 21x + 108$ (v) $x^2 + 3\sqrt{3}\,x + 6$

(vi) $(a^2 - 2a)^2 - 23(a^2 - 2a) + 120.$ (vii) $x^4 - 5x^2 + 4$

(viii) $(x^2 - 4x)(x^2 - 4x - 1) - 20$

32. The scatter plot below shows the average points scored per game by players of different ages in an adult basketball league.

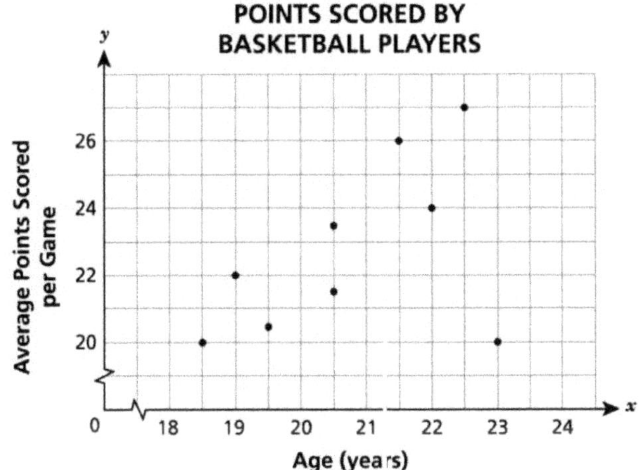

Which statement **best** describes the association between a player's age, in years, and the average points scored per game?

A   There is no association.

B   There is a nonlinear association.

C   There is a positive linear association and one outlier.

D   There is a negative linear association and one outlier.

33. If $x^2 + px + q = (x + a)(x + b)$, then factorize $x^2 + pxy + qy^2$

34. Factorize each of the following expressions:

(i) $\sqrt{3}\, x^2 + 11x + 6\sqrt{3}$

(ii) $4\sqrt{3}\, x^2 + 5x - 2\sqrt{3}$

(iii) $7\sqrt{2}\, x^2 - 10x - 4\sqrt{2}$

35. Sum total of square of a number and its reciprocal is equal to 16.25. Find the sum total of cube and square of the number.

36. What fraction of all the whole numbers up to 300 are multiples of 29?

37. Half of a quarter of 72064 + one nineteenth of 57,095 = ...

38. In city W, the average cost for a gym membership is given by the equation
$y = 34.99x + 49$, where y is the total cost, in dollars, for x months of membership.
What is the meaning of the y-value when $x = 1$?

A   the average sign-up fee for a gym membership

B   the average monthly charge for a gym membership

C   the average total cost for the first month of a gym membership

D   the average total cost for the first two months of a gym membership

39. What is the volume, in terms of π, for a cylindrical container with a radius of
3.25 centimeters and a height of 10 centimeters?

40. Mya claims $(m\angle 3 + m\angle 4) = m\angle 1$, as shown in the triangle below.

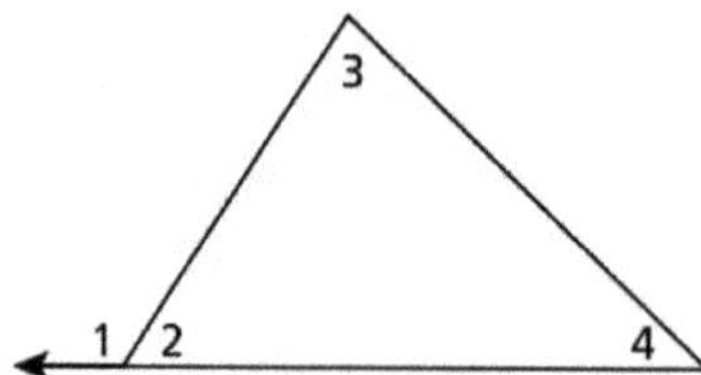

Which equations explain why Mya's claim must be true?

A $(m\angle 1 + m\angle 2) = 90°$ and $(m\angle 3 + m\angle 4) = 90°$

B $(m\angle 1 + m\angle 2) = 180°$ and $(m\angle 3 + m\angle 4) = 180°$

C $(m\angle 1 + m\angle 2) = 90°$ and $(m\angle 3 + m\angle 4 + m\angle 2) = 90°$

D $(m\angle 1 + m\angle 2) = 180°$ and $(m\angle 3 + m\angle 4 + m\angle 2) = 180°$

41. Two cells are viewed and measured under a microscope. The approximate diameter
of each cell is listed below.

- cell P: 5.0×10^{-4} meters

- cell Q: 3.0×10^{-5} meters

What is the approximate difference, in meters, between the diameter of cell P and
the diameter of cell Q?

A 2.0×10^{-5} **C** 4.7×10^{-5}

B 2.0×10^{-4} **D** 4.7×10^{-4}

42. What fraction of all the numbers starting from 101 to 200 are multiples of 102?

Combined Evaluation II

01. A function of x is shown on the coordinate plane.

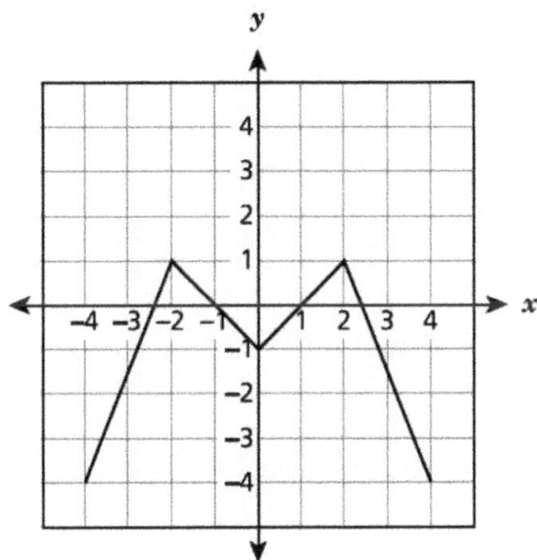

Over which intervals is the function increasing?

A $-4 < x < -2$ and $-1 < x < 1$ **C** $-2 < x < 0$ and $2 < x < 4$

B $-4 < x < -2$ and $0 < x < 2$ **D** $-2 < x < -1$ and $2 < x < 4$

2. If $x + \dfrac{9}{x} = 3$, then find the following:

$a)\ x^6 - 27$ $b)\ x^2 - \dfrac{81}{x^2}$ $c)\ x^3 - \dfrac{27}{x^3}$

3. Sum total of the cube root of a number x and reciprocal of x is equal to 2.125. Find the value of the following:

a) $x^3 - 27$ a) $x^2 - 64$ a) $(x^3 - 9)(x^3 + 9)$ a) $x^4 - 625$

4. $x^2 + 11x + 121 = \dfrac{1332}{x-11}$. Find the value of $x^3 + \dfrac{1}{x^3}$

5. $11x^2 + 66x - 7 = 0$. Find the value of $\dfrac{x+7}{11x-1}$

6. Complete the following:

#	Expression	Answer
1.	$4^5 \cdot 4^{-4} =$	
2.	$4^5 \cdot 4^{-3} =$	
3.	$4^5 \cdot 4^{-2} =$	
4.	$7^{-4} \cdot 7^{11} =$	
5.	$7^{-4} \cdot 7^{10} =$	
6.	$7^{-4} \cdot 7^9 =$	
7.	$9^{-4} \cdot 9^{-3} =$	
8.	$9^{-4} \cdot 9^{-2} =$	
9.	$9^{-4} \cdot 9^{-1} =$	
10.	$9^{-4} \cdot 9^0 =$	
11.	$5^0 \cdot 5^1 =$	
12.	$5^0 \cdot 5^2 =$	
13.	$5^0 \cdot 5^3 =$	
14.	$(12^3)^9 =$	
15.	$(12^3)^{10} =$	
16.	$(12^3)^{11} =$	
17.	$(7^{-3})^{-8} =$	
18.	$(7^{-3})^{-9} =$	
19.	$(7^{-3})^{-10} =$	
20.	$\left(\frac{1}{2}\right)^9 =$	
21.	$\left(\frac{1}{2}\right)^8 =$	
22.	$\left(\frac{1}{2}\right)^7 =$	
23.	$\left(\frac{1}{2}\right)^6 =$	
24.	$(3x)^5 =$	
25.	$(3x)^7 =$	
26.	$(3x)^9 =$	
27.	$(8^{-2})^3 =$	
28.	$(8^{-3})^3 =$	
29.	$(8^{-4})^3 =$	
30.	$(22^0)^{50} =$	
31.	$(22^0)^{55} =$	
32.	$(22^0)^{60} =$	
33.	$\left(\frac{1}{11}\right)^{-5} =$	
34.	$\left(\frac{1}{11}\right)^{-6} =$	
35.	$\left(\frac{1}{11}\right)^{-7} =$	
36.	$\dfrac{56^{-23}}{56^{-34}} =$	
37.	$\dfrac{87^{-12}}{87^{-34}} =$	
38.	$\dfrac{23^{-15}}{23^{-17}} =$	
39.	$(-2)^{-12} \cdot (-2)^1 =$	
40.	$\dfrac{2y}{y^3} =$	
41.	$\dfrac{5xy^7}{15x^7y} =$	
42.	$\dfrac{16x^6y^9}{8x^{-5}y^{-11}} =$	
43.	$(2^3 \cdot 4)^{-5} =$	
44.	$(9^{-8})(27^{-2}) =$	

7. Is the following expression a polynomial?

$$x^9 + 121x^8 + x^{4\frac{5}{}} + 101x^{-9} + \frac{x^3}{9} + 3x^{-3} + 2x^7 + 1001$$

8. If $a^2 + b^2 + c^2 = 24$ and ab + bc + ac = - 4, then find the value of a + b + c.

9. If (x + y + z) = 0, then find the value of $(x + y)^3 + (y + z)^3 + (z + x)^3$.

10. A fish tank is in the form of a cuboid, external measures of that cuboid are 80 cm ×40 cm ×30 cm. The base, side faces and back face are to be covered with a coloured paper. Find the area of the paper needed in cm^2

11. The dimensions of a Cinema Hall are 100 m, 60 m and 15 m. How many person can sit in the hall, if each requires 150 m^3 of air ?

12. A cylindrical container with internal radius of its base 10 cm, contains water up to a height of 7 cm. Find the area of the wet surface of the cylinder.

13. A godown measures 40m × 25m × 10m. Find the maximum number of wooden crates each measuring 1.5m × 1.25m × 0.5m that can be stored in the godown.

14. If the perimeter of each face of a cube is 32cm, find its lateral surface area. Note that four faces which meet the base of a cube are called its lateral faces.

15. if V is the volume of a cuboid of dimensions a, b, c and S is its surface area, then prove that

$$\frac{1}{V} = \frac{2}{S}(\frac{1}{a} + \frac{1}{b} + \frac{1}{c})$$

13. half of a, quarter of b and one eighth of c are equal to each other. Find ratio of the following: $(a^3 + b^3 + c^3)$: 3abc

14. Factorize the followings

a. $3x^2 - 7x - 6$ b. $16x^2 - 12x - 10$

c. $36x^4 - 229x^2 + 25$ d. $6x^2 - 3xy + 11x - 4y + 4$

e. $10a^2 + 3b^2 + 17ab - 22a - 7b + 4$

f. $4x^2 + 2xy - 2y^2 + 13xz - 5yz + 3z^2$

g. $3x^2 - 2xy - 20xz + 14yz - 7z^2$

15. Water in a canal 30dm wide and 12dm deep, is flowing with a velocity of 100km per hour. How much area will it irrigate in 30 minutes, if 8cm of standing water is desired?

16. Find the edge of a cube whose surface area is 432m^2.

17. A cylinder and a cone have equal radii of their bases and equal heights. If their curved surface areas are in the ratio 8 : 5, show that the radius of each is to the height of each as 3 : 4.

18. The dimensions of a rectangular box are in the ratio of 2 : 3 : 4 and the difference between the cost of covering it with sheet of paper at the rates of Rs. 8 and Rs. 9.50 per m^2 is Rs. 1248. Find the dimensions of the box,

19. The areas of three adjacent faces of a cuboid are x. y. z. If the volume is V , prove that $V^2 = xyz$

20. Three cubes of each side 4cm are joined end to end. Find the surface area of the resulting cuboid.

21. A swimming pool is 50 metres long and 15 metes wide and 15 meters wide. Its shallow and deep ends are $1\frac{1}{2}$ meters and $4\frac{1}{2}$ meters deep respectively.If the bottom of the pool slopes uniformly, find the amount of water required to fill the pool.

22. The radius and height of a cylinder are in the ration 3 : 2 and its volume is 19404 cm 3. Find its radius and height.

23. The inner dimensions of a closed wooden box are 2 m, 1.2 m and 0.75 m. The thickness of the wood is 2.5 cm. Find the cost of wood required to make the box if $1m^3$ of wood costs Rs 5400.

24. Find the prime factorisation of the following numbers:
$100^3 - 49^3 + 10^3 - 61^3$

25. Find the prime factoristion of the following numbers:
$30^3 - 12^3 - 10^3 - 8^3$

26. Factorise: $3x^2 + 6x + 6$

27. Factorise: $2p(x + y) - 3q(x + y)$

28. Factorise:
a) $3x^3 + 5x^2 + 3x + 5$ b) $3x^4 + 6x^3y + 9x^2$ c) $5pq + 20p^3q^3 - 15p^2q$

29. Solve: $8x^2 - 72xy + 12x$

30. Find integers 'a' and 'b' such that $(x^2 - x - 1)$ divides $ax^{17} + bx^{16} + 1$.

31. Factorise $4x^2 + 4\sqrt{3}x + 3 = 0$.

32. Factorize $\dfrac{1}{6}a^2 - a + \dfrac{4}{3}$.

33. Solve:

$$5(2x+1)(3x+5) \div (2x+1)$$

34. Simplify : $\dfrac{(3x^2 - 24x + 36)(x - 4)}{3(x^2 - 6x - 8)}$

35. $(p^2 + 5p + 4) \div (p + 1)$

36. Factorize the following.

$$ax^2y + bxy^2 + cxyz.$$

37. Factorize the following algebraic expression.

$$(a + 7)(a - 10) + 16.$$

38. If $x = (2 + \sqrt{5})^{\frac{1}{3}} + (2 - \sqrt{5})^{\frac{1}{3}}$ and $y = (2 + \sqrt{5})^{\frac{1}{3}} - (2 - \sqrt{5})^{\frac{1}{3}}$, then

evaluate $x^2 + y^2$.

The $p(x) = ax^3 = 3x^2 + 4a$ and $2x^3 - 5x + a$ when divided by $(x - 2)$ leaves the remainder p and q. If $p - 2q = 4$, find a

39. Divide $\sqrt{2}a^3 + 3\sqrt{2}a^2 + 6a$ by $2a$.

40. Factorise:

$$x^2 + 20x - 69$$

39. If $303.606 \div 101 =$ P and $19.038 \div 19 =$ Q, then

Statements:

    a. Both P and Q are decimal numbers having values up to thousandths place.

    b. Value of $\dfrac{(P+Q)}{(P-Q)}$ is a natural number.

    c. Sum total of P and Q estimated to nearest tenths is also a natural number.

    d. $\dfrac{P}{Q} - \dfrac{Q}{P}$ returns a value, which lies between 3 and 4.

    e. Fraction $\dfrac{P}{Q}$ has denominator 2.

Which of the above statements regarding values of P and Q cannot be finalised?

Options: A: c, d and e   B: Only d   C: b, c and e   D: a and b

40. Which of the following is/are true?

    (i) $A = B + C$

    (ii) A is the greatest digit integer

    (iii) $C = 0$

$$
\begin{array}{cccc}
  & A & A & A \\
+ & B & B & B \\
+ & C & C & C \\
\hline
B & A & A & C \\
\end{array}
$$

41. Solve the following:

A. If $x^2 + y^2 + xy = 1$ and $x + y = 2$, then find xy.

    (a) -3 (b) 3

    (c) $-\dfrac{3}{2}$ (d) $-\dfrac{2}{3}$

B. Factorization of the polynomial

$11x^2 - 10\sqrt{3}x - 3$ gives __________.

    (a) $\left(x + \sqrt{3}\right)\left(11x - \sqrt{3}\right)$

    (b) $\left(x + 3\sqrt{3}\right)\left(11x - \sqrt{3}\right)$

    (c) $\left(x - \sqrt{3}\right)\left(11x + \sqrt{3}\right)$

    (d) $\left(x + \sqrt{3}\right)\left(11x + \sqrt{3}\right)$

C. If $h(y) = y^2$ and $g(z) = z^3$, then the HCF of $h(b) - h(a)$ and $g(b) - g(a)$ is __________.

    (a) $a + b$

    (b) $a^2 - b^2$

    (c) $b - a$

    (d) $a - b$

D. The HCF of the polynomials $(x^3 - 9^3)\,(x + 3)$ and $(x^2 - 9)\,(x^2 - 3)$ is __________.

    (a) $x + \sqrt{3}$

    (b) $x - 9$

    (c) $x + 3$

    (d) $x - 3$

42. What least number can be subtracted from five digit smallest multiple of 9 to make it a square number?

43. Simplify: $\left(1 + \dfrac{1}{2}\right)\left(1 + \dfrac{1}{3}\right) \dots \left(1 + \dfrac{1}{1{,}000}\right) X\ 202 = $ ... .

44. Somalwar paints a wall in 7 days while working alone at the rate of 8 hours a day. Find the number of days required for finishing painting of four such walls while working 7 hours a day.

45. Answer the following:

A. The polynomial $x^2 + y^2 - z^2 - 2xy$ on factorization gives __________.

(a) $(x - y - z)(x - y + z)$

(b) $(x + y + z)(x - y + z)$

(c) $(x + y + z)(x - y - z)$

(d) $(x - y + z)(x + y - z)$

B. The polynomial $x^3 + 8y^3 + 27z^3 - 18xyz$ on factorization gives __________.

(a) $(x + 2y + 3z)(x^2 + 4y^2 + 9z^2 + 2xy + 6yz + 3zx)$

(b) $(x + 2y + 3z)(x^2 + 4y^2 + 9z^2 + 4xy + 12yz + 6zx)$

(c) $(x + 2y + 3z)(x^2 + 4y^2 + 9z^2 - 2xy - 6yz - 3zx)$

(d) $(x + 2y + 3z)(x^2 + 4y^2 + 9z^2 - 2xy - 12yz - 6zx)$

C. The factors of the expression

$a + b + c + 2\sqrt{ab} - 2\sqrt{bc} - 2\sqrt{ca}$ are __________.

(a) $\sqrt{a} - \sqrt{b} + \sqrt{c}, \sqrt{a} - \sqrt{b} + \sqrt{c}$

(b) $\sqrt{a} + \sqrt{b} - \sqrt{c}, \sqrt{a} - \sqrt{b} + \sqrt{c}$

(c) $\sqrt{a} + \sqrt{b} - \sqrt{c}, \sqrt{a} + \sqrt{b} - \sqrt{c}$

(d) $\sqrt{a} + \sqrt{b} - \sqrt{c}, \sqrt{a} + b - c$

D. The HCF of two polynomials A and B using long division method was found to be $2x + 1$ after two steps. The first two quotients obtained are x and $(x + 1)$. Find A and B. Given that degree of $A >$ degree of B.

(a) $A = 2x^3 + 3x^2 + x - 1, B = 2x^2 - 3x + 1$

(b) $A = 2x^3 - 3x^2 + x - 1, B = 2x^2 - 3x - 1$

(c) $A = 2x^3 + 3x^2 - 3x - 1, B = 2x^2 - 3x + 1$

46. Answer the following:

A. The HCF of $(x - 1)(x^2 - 4)$ and $(x^2 - 1)(x + 2)$ is __________.

(a) $x - 2$ (b) $x + 1$

(c) $x - 1$ (d) $(x - 1)(x + 2)$

B. The HCF and LCM of the polynomials $p(x)$ and $q(x)$ are $(x^2 + 2x)(x^2 - 20x + 91)$ and $2x^2(x^2 - 2x - 143)(x^2 - 5x - 14)$. If $p(x)$ is $x(x - 13)(x - 7)(x^2 + 13x + 22)$, then $q(x)$ is __________.

(a) $2x^2(x^2 - 20x + 91)(x - 2)$

(b) $2x^2(x - 9)^2(x - 11)$

(c) $2x^2(x^2 - 20x + 91)(x + 2)$

(d) $2x^2(x^2 + 20x - 91)(x + 2)$

C. The LCM of the polynomials $(x - 3)(x + 5)^2$, $(x + 5)(x - 7)^2$ and $(x - 7)(x - 3)^2$ is __________.

D. If the LCM of the polynomials $(x - 3)(x - p)$ and $(x + 3)(x + 5)$ is $(x - 3)(x + 3)(x - p)$, then p is __________.

(a) -5 (b) -4

(c) -2 (d) -1

E. The number of terms which contain variables in the expansion of $\left(x + \dfrac{1}{x} + 1\right)^2$ is __________.

(a) 6   (b) 5

(c) 4   (d) 3

F. If $(a + b + c)^2 = 36$, $ab + bc + ca = 11$ and $a, b, c \in N$, then find $a^2 + b^2 + c^2$.

(a) 17   (b) 22

(c) 14   (d) 6

47. Complete the following: If three digits are different then three digits can be arranged in six different ways Number of four digit numbers are

$$9.10.10.10 - 9.9.8.7 - 9.9.8(6) = 9000 - 4536 - 3888 = \ldots\ldots$$

48. Given condition:

Number × Sum of the Digits = 405

Now, factors of 405 will give the required number.

Factors of $405 = 5 \times 3 \times 3 \times 3 \times 3 = 15 \times 27 = 45 \times 9$

$45 \times 9 = \ldots\ldots$ Also, $54 \times 9 = \ldots\ldots\ldots$

So, Required number $= \ldots\ldots\ldots$

49. Solve the following:

A. If $a + b + c = 6$ and $\dfrac{1}{a} + \dfrac{1}{b} + \dfrac{1}{c} = \dfrac{3}{2}$, then find

$$\frac{a}{b} + \frac{a}{c} + \frac{b}{a} + \frac{b}{c} + \frac{c}{a} + \frac{c}{b}.$$

(a) 6　　　　　　　　(b) 4

(c) 9　　　　　　　　(d) 12

B. If $\left(\dfrac{a}{b}\right) + \left(\dfrac{b}{a}\right) = 2$, then find $\left(\dfrac{a}{b}\right)^{10} - \left(\dfrac{b}{a}\right)^{10}$.

(a) $\dfrac{2^{20} - 1}{2^{10}}$　　　　　(b) 2

(c) 0　　　　　　　(d) $\dfrac{2^{20} + 1}{2^{10}}$

C. $x^4 + y^4 - x^2 y^2 = $ _______

(a) $(x^2 + y^2 + \sqrt{3}\ xy)(x^2 + y^2 - \sqrt{3}\ xy)$

D. If $p(x) = (x - 4)^p (x + 6)^5$, $q(x) = (x + 6)^q (x - 4)^6$ and LCM of $p(x)$ and $q(x)$ is $(x - 4)^6 (x + 6)^q$, then find the maximum value of $(p - q)$.

(a) -1　　　　　　(b) 0

(c) 1　　　　　　　(d) 11

E. If $x^2 + y^2 - xy = 3$ and $y - x = 1$, then find $\dfrac{xy}{x^2 + y^2}$.

(a) $\dfrac{2}{5}$　　　　　　(b) $\dfrac{5}{2}$

(c) $\dfrac{3}{5}$　　　　　　(d) $\dfrac{5}{3}$

F. If $abc = 6$ and $a + b + c = 6$, then find the value of $\dfrac{1}{ac} + \dfrac{1}{ab} + \dfrac{1}{bc}$.

50. Select correct options:

A. In $r_1 = \dfrac{A}{s - a}$, if $A = 12$ cm^2, $r_1 = 4$ cm, and $a = 3$ cm, then find s making s as the subject.

(a) 6 cm　　　　　　(b) 8 cm

(c) 12 cm　　　　　(d) 16 cm

B. In the formula $v = u + at$, if $a = 5$ m/s^2, $t = 3$ s and $v = 20$ m/s, then $u = $ _______ .

(a) 10 m/s　　　　　(b) 6 m/s

(c) 7 m/s　　　　　(d) 5 m/s

C. Write all the auxiliary formulae related to $x^2 - y^2 = z^2$.

(a) $x = \sqrt{y^2 + z^2}$, $y = \sqrt{x^2 - z^2}$, and $z = \sqrt{x^2 - y^2}$

(b) $x = \sqrt{z^2 + y^2}$, $y = \sqrt{z^2 - x^2}$, and $z^2 = \sqrt{x^2 - y^2}$

(c) $x = \sqrt{y^2 + z^2}$, $y = \sqrt{x^2 - z^2}$, and $z = \sqrt{y^2 - x^2}$

D. Frame the formula: Sum of the products of p, x and q, y is equal to r.

(a) $py + qx = r$　　　　(b) $px - qy = r$

(c) $px + qy = r$　　　　(d) $px + qy + r = 0$

E. If $t_n = a\, r^{n-1}$, then find the value of n, given that $a = 2$, $r = 3$, and $t_n = 486$.

(a) 5　　　　　　　(b) 6

(c) 4　　　　　　　(d) 8

F. If $\dfrac{1}{x} + \dfrac{1}{y} = \dfrac{1}{z} + \dfrac{1}{w}$, then make w as the subject of the formula.

(a) $w = \dfrac{xyz}{xy + 9yz + zx}$　　　(b) $w = \dfrac{xyz}{yz + zx - xy}$

51. Half of a quarter of 16,080 + quarter of one sixth of 24,120 = ... X 1,005

52. If $9x^2 + 12x + 5 = 0$ then find the value of $x^3 - 9$.

53. Length and breadth of a rectangle is in the ratio of 1:3. Area of rectangle is 4,963 sq. cm. Find outer boundary of that rectangle.

54. What fraction of all the numbers starting from 1 to 1,000 are multiples of 99?

55. Find the greatest three digit multiple of 11 which is also divisible by 2 and 4.

56. Answer the following:

A. There is a natural number which becomes equal to the square of a natural number when 100 is added to it, and to the square of another natural number when 168 is added to it. Find the number.

B. Find the two-digit number if the number of its units exceeds by 2 the number of its tens and the product of the required number, by the sum of its digits is equal to 144.

C. Subtract the number obtained by reversing the digits of the number 20198 from the number obtained by interchanging the digits in the unit's place and the hundred's place of the same number, we get

________.

D. In the following, find the digits represented by the letters:

$$
\begin{array}{r}
3\,A \\
\times\ A \\
\hline
2\,B\,A
\end{array}
$$

E. Write the following numbers in generalised form:
39, 52, 106, 359, 628, 3458, 9502, 7000

F. Call a natural number n faithful, if there exist numbers $a < b < c$ such that a divides b, b divides c and $n = a + b + c$. Show that all but a finite number of natural numbers are faithful. Find the sum of all natural numbers which are not faithful.

G. Suppose a 3 digit number abc is divisible by 3. Prove that abc + bca + cab is divisible by 9.

57. If $x2 + x + 1 = 0$, then find the value of $(x^{100} - x^{99} + x^{98} - x^{97} \, \text{---} \, + x^2 - x)$

58. Cistern A can fill up an empty tank in 50 minutes and cistern B can fill it up in 1 h 40 minutes. If both the cisterns kept open then find the time taken by these cisterns to fill up four such water tanks.

59. Due to price rise a family reduced the consumption of cooking oil by 24% to keep the monthly expenditure on cooking oil unchanged. Find the rice rise in percentage.

Combined Evaluation III

1. Capacity of three cans is in the ratio of 1:2:3. Smallest can holds 200 ml less than a liter of any liquid. Find capacity of all the cans.
2. Find the value of x if $x^2 + x + 1 = 0$. Consider value of x as positive. [hints: $(x^3 - 1) = (x-1)(x^2 + x + 1)$;
3. Find the two largest numbers of four digits having 531 as their HCF.

4. Find the value of q.

$$64 X 56 - \sqrt[3]{q} = 128 X 24$$

5. If

$$\sqrt[2]{2^n} = 16, \ then \ n = \ \_\_\_\_$$

6. 15 men, 18 women and 12 boys working together earned Rs 2070. If the daily wages of a man, a woman and a boy are in the ratio 4 : 3 : 2, the daily wages (in Rs) of 1 man, 2 women and 3 boys are ___________.

7. Bolton started business investing Rs 8000. Three months later John joined him investing Rs 6000. If they make a profit of Rs 5100 at the end of the year, how much should be John's share ?

8. The employer reduces the number of employees in the ratio 9 : 8 and increases their wages in the ratio 14 : 15. If the previous wage bill was Rs 189000, what is the amount by which the new wage bill will increase or decrease ?

9. Rs 2010 are to be divided among A, B and C in such a way that if A gets Rs 5, than B must get Rs 12 and if B gets Rs 4, then C must get Rs 5.50. The share of C will exceed that of B by __________.

10. Find the ratio of 12% 0f 12 and 15% of 15.

11. What least number must be added to 1968 to make it divisible by 11?

12. A bottle is full of spirit. One-third of it is taken out and then an equal amount of water is poured into the bottle to fill it. This operation is done four times. Find the final ratio of spirit and water in the bottle.

13. The students in three classes are in the ratio 2 : 3 : 5. If 40 students are increased in each class, the ratio changes to 4 : 5 : 7. Originally the total number of students was ____________.

14. Find the least number which when divided by 12, 24, 36 and 40 leaves a remainder 1, but when divided by 7 leaves no remainder.

15. A drum contains 20 l of a paint. From this, 2 l of paint is taken out and replaced by 2 l of oil. Again 2 l of this mixture is taken out and replaced by 2 l of oil. If this operation is performed once again, then what would be the final ratio of paint and oil in the drum ?

16. 100 ml 80% alcohol and 150 ml 90% alcohol mixed up properly to make a new combination having strength _______ %.

17. Concentrations of three solutions A, B and C are 20%, 30% and 40% respectively. They are mixed in the ratio 3 : 5 : x resulting in a solution of 30% concentration. Find x.

18. Ratio of incomes of A, B and C last year was 3 : 4 : 5. The ratios of their individual incomes of last year and this year are 4 : 5, 2 : 3 and 3 : 4 respectively. If the sum of their present incomes is Rs 78800. Find the present individual income of B.

19. Ravi earns 25% more than Nisha, gut his earning is 18% less than that of Faquir. Find the ratio of their earnings.

20. The cost of manufacturing a TV set is made up of material costs, labour costs and overhead costs. These costs are in the ratio 4 : 3 : 2. If materials costs and labour costs rise by 10% and 8% respectively, while the overhead costs reduce by 5%, what is the percentage increase in the total cost of the TV set ?

21. A number is increased by 20% and then again by 20%. By what per cent should the increased number be reduced so as to get back the original number ?

22. The number of employees working in a farm is increased by 25% and the wages per head are decreased by 25%. If it results in x% decrease in total wages, then the value of x is ___________.

23. A candidate who gets 20% marks in an examination fails by 30 marks but another candidate who gets 32%, gets 42 marks more than the pass marks. The percentage of pass marks is __________.

24. In the expression xy2 , the values of both variables x and y are decreased by 20%. By this the value of the expression will be decreased by ___________________.

25. In an examination Nancy obtained 20% more marks than Hary but are 10% less than Della. If the marks obtained by Hary are 1080, find the percentage of marks obtained by Nancy, if the full marks are 2000.

26. A student took five papers in an examination, where the full marks were the same for each papers, this marks in these papers were in the proportion 6 : 7 : 8 : 9 : 10. In all the papers together, the candidate obtained 60% of the total marks. Then, the number of papers in which he got more than 50% marks is equal to ___________________.

27. A tax payer is exempted of income tax for the first Rs 100000 of his annual income but for the rest of the income, he has to pay a tax at the rate of 20%. If he paid Rs 3160 as income tax for a year, his monthly income is _________________

28. A house-owner was having his house painted. He was advised that he would require 25 kg of paint. Allowing for 15% wastage and assuming that the paint is available in 2 kg cans, what would be the cost of paint purchased, if one can costs $ 2 ?

29. By receiving 5% less vote than the winner of a by-election a candidate received only 12% of the total vote. Find the ration of votes received by both the candidate.

30. In an election, 10% of the people in the voter's list did not participate. 60 votes were declared invalid. There are only two candidates A and B. A defeated B by 308 votes. It has found that 47% of the people listed in the voters' list voted for A. Find the total number of votes polled.

31. Prices register an increase of 10% on food grains and 15% on other items of expenditure. If the ratio of an employee's expenditure on food grains and other items be 2 : 5, by how much should his salary be increased in order that he may maintain the same level of consumption as before, his present salary being Rs 2590.

32. What is the least number which when divided by the numbers 3, 5, 6, 8, 10 and 12 leaves in each case a remainder 2, but when divided by 13 leaves no remainder.

33. Find the value of p. $144 X\, 36 \; - \; \sqrt[3]{p} \; = \; 72 X\, 48$

34. What fraction of a fortnight is an hour?

35. Half a cup sugar measures 130 g. There are ______________ cups of sugar in 5.2 kg pack of sugar.

36. Here m = _____

$$\sqrt[4]{\sqrt[5]{\sqrt[6]{p^8}}} \; = \; p^m$$

37. Prices register an increase of 10% on food grains and 15% on other items of expenditure. If the ratio of an employee's expenditure on food grains and other items be 2 : 5, by how much should his salary be increased in order that he may maintain the same level of consumption as before, his present salary being Rs 2590.

38. 10% of 29 is _______ less than 5% of 300.

39. A sold a watch to B at 20% gain and B sold it to C at a loss of 10%. If C bought the watch for Rs 216, at what price did A purchase it ?

40. A man sold two steel chairs for Rs 500 each. On one, he gains 20% and on the other he loss 12%. How much does he gain or loss in the whole transaction ?

41. Three items are purchased at $ 450 each. One of them is sold at a loss of 10%. At what price should the other two be sold so as to gain 20% on the whole transaction? What is the gain% on these two items?

42. A scale of thermometer developed in such a way that water boils at 90^0 and water freezes at 10^0. What temperature of atmosphere will be represented by that thermometer when it is 35^0 C outside?

Options:

I.   Fundamental interval in accord to newly graduated thermometer will be 0.8.

II.   There will be 0.8^0 increase in the new scale for a corresponding increase of 1^0 C.

III.   For calculating the temperature correspond to the Celsius scale we simply divide the reading of the new scale with its fundamental interval.

IV.   Lower Fixed Point of new scale is at its 10^0 mark and upper Fixed Point is at 90^0 mark. Fundamental interval of this scale duly calculated is 0.8.

     Any one of the above statement is not true. Which one of the above statements is not true?

A: II   B: III   C: IV   D: V

Combined Evaluation IV

1. P = 515.15 –15.51–1.51–5.11– 1.11.

   Find the value of 2P + 1

2. If a = (7.5 × 7.5 + 37.5 + 2.5 × 2.5), then find the value of

   $$\frac{a^2+1}{a^2-1} - \frac{a^2-1}{a^2+1}$$

3. A began a business with Rs 45000 and B joined after wards with Rs 30000. At the end of a year, the profit is divided in the ratio 2:1. When did B join ?

4. An employer reduces the number of his employees in the ratio 7: 5 and increases their wages in the ratio 15 : 28. State whether his bill of total wages increase or decrease and in what ratio.

5. In three vessels, the ratio of water and milk is 6 : 7, 5 : 9 and 8 : 7 respectively. If the mixtures of the three vessels are mixed together, then what will be the ratio of water and milk ?

6. A drum contains 20 litres of a paint. From this, 2 litres of paint is taken out and replaced by 2 litres of oil. Again 2 litres of this mixture is taken out and replaced by 2 litres of oil. If this operation is performed once again, then what would be the final ratio of paint and oil in the drum ?

7. If a : (b + c) = 1 : 3 and c : (a + b) = 5 : 7, then b : (a + c) = ____ .

8. 15 men, 18 women and 12 boys working together earned Rs 2070. If the daily wages of a man, a woman and a boy are in the ratio 4 : 3 : 2, the daily wages (in Rs) of 1 man, 2 women and 3 boys are _________________.

9. Ratio of the incomes of A, B and C last year was 3 : 4 : 5. The ratio of their individual incomes during the last year and this year are 4 : 5, 2 : 3 and 3 : 4 respectively. If the sum of their present incomes is Rs 78800, then find the present individual income of A, B and C.

10. 10% of A = 20% of B = 30% of C. Find the value $\dfrac{AB+BC+AC}{ABC}$.

11. $\dfrac{1}{10}$ of a number x exceeds $\dfrac{1}{15}$ of another number y by 5. Find the value of P.

$$P = \dfrac{3x-2y}{3x+2y} + \dfrac{3x+2y}{3x-2y} .$$

12. Tap A can fill a tank in 30 minutes and tap B can fill the same tank in 40 minutes. Both the tap can fill the tank jointly in _____ mins.

13. In two alloys, copper and zinc are related in the ratio of 4 : 1 and 1 : 3. 10 kg of 1st alloy, 16 kg of 2nd alloy and some of pure copper are melted together. An alloy was obtained in which the ratio of copper to zinc was 3 : 2. Find the weight of the new alloy ?

14. Railway fares of 1st, 2nd and 3rd classes between two stations were in the ratio 8 : 6 : 3. The fares of 1st and 2nd class were subsequently reduced by $\dfrac{1}{6}$ and $\dfrac{1}{12}$ respectively. If during a year, the ratio between the passengers of 1st, 2nd and 3rd classes was 9 : 12 : 26 and the total amount collected by the sale of tickets was Rs 1088, the collection from the passengers of 1st class was _____________.

15. Salary of Mark is increased by 16%. His previous salary was _____ % less than that of the increased salary.

16. Solve the following equation :

$$\frac{11}{144} X \frac{12}{169} X \frac{13}{121} X \frac{132}{341} X \frac{682}{1001} X \frac{13}{19} =$$

17. What least number must added to the smallest six digit number and must be subtracted from the largest five digit number to make both of them a multiple of 11?

18. What least number must be added to 121.098 to make it a multiple of 1.001?

19. First tap can fill a water tank in 30 minutes and second tap can empty the half filled tank in 1.5 hours. By what time the empty tank will be filled up if both the tap kept open?

20. Half of a cake is given to all friends, half of the remaining portion of the cake retained by parents, one third of what remaining was distributed amongst John's classmates. Finally John received only 200 g of the cake. Find the quantity of that cake.

21. How many different possible solutions can satisfy the following equation?

$$(x^2 - 5x + 5)^{(x^2-12x+45)} = 1$$

22. A three digit number is such that the number N = 100a + 10b + c. Again the number is a product of two factors b and 10c + b. Find the number.

23. An integer is a palindrome when the same number is obtained when digits are reversed. 121,253, 132 etc. are all palindromes. Find a number n such that n^2 will be a palindrome with 6 digits.

24. Sum of the digits of a smallest possible number N is 18. Sum total of all the digits of 2N is 27. Find out the value of N.

25. What least number must be added to a six digit smallest number to make the number 1210214 divisible by 74.

26. Evaluate the following.

$$\left(\sqrt{2} + \sqrt{11} + \sqrt{13}\right)\left(\sqrt{2} + \sqrt{11} - \sqrt{13}\right)\left(\sqrt{2} - \sqrt{11} + \sqrt{13}\right)$$

$$\left(-\sqrt{2} + \sqrt{11} - \sqrt{13}\right)$$

27. Each interior angles of a heptagon is obtuse. Angles are multiples of 9. Find the degrees of sums of the two largest angles.

28. A three digit number is multiplied by 3 and 1 added to it then the result is a reverse of the original number. Find the original number.

[Hints:

(100 a+ 10b + c)X3 +1 = 100c + 10b + a .

100 a+ 10b + c = ?]

29. If ab $= a^b$ and $\dfrac{a}{b} = a^{3b}$, find b^{-a}

30. $0.33 < \dfrac{m}{n} < \dfrac{1}{3}$. Find the smallest possible value of n to satisfy the above mentioned relationship.

31. Find the smallest seven digit number which is divisible by 11. What are the two digits will be there in tens and ones place of that number?

32. Mark deposited $ 23,500 in his savings bank account which was offering 4% simple interest per year. Find the amount that Mark will obtain after a tenure of 4 years and 5 months.

33. -4.5 + 5.64 + _______ = 0. Make this equation true.

34. Solve the following

    a. $7 \times 20 - 2 \times 4 + 3^2 + 12 \div 4$

b. $\dfrac{\left(\sqrt[3]{0.125}+\sqrt[2]{.0064}\right)}{\sqrt[3]{1.331}-\sqrt[2]{0.0081}}$

c. If $x + \dfrac{1}{x} = 9$ then find the value of

$$(2x - 9)^2$$

35. A shopkeeper purchased 16 dozen bananas at the rate of Rs 24 per dozen and found that 5% of his stock became non sellable. Rest of his stock was sold at the rate of Rs 30 per dozen. Find out the rate percent of his gain or loss incurred in this business.

36. Simplify the following:

$7[120 - 2(4 + 3)^2 + 12] \div 2$

37. X = 0.3333... + 0.4444 + 0.9999.. Find the value of $\dfrac{x+1}{x-1} + \dfrac{x-1}{x+1}$

38. Shweta joined a Yoga Centre and her body weight was reduced from 76 kg to 65.6 kg. Find the percentage weight loss that she made during the tenure of her exercises.

39. Base of a triangle is reduced by 5% and its height is increased by 5%. Find the total percentage increase or decrease in the area of the triangle.

40. All the five sides of a regular pentagon is 12 cm each and apothem is 8 cm. find the area of this pentagon.

   [Hints: The apothem of a regular polygon is a line segment from the center of the polygon perpendicular to a side.]

41. A ___________ angle is an angle with its vertex at the center of a circle whose sides are radii.

42. Calculate the total surface area of a cuboidal room of dimension 8mX6mX5m.

125

43. Arrange the following values in ascending and descending order:

44. What is the next number in the following sequence: 2, 4, 8, 16, _______, _______ ?

45. Write 3/7 and 5/9 in their corresponding decimal form. What are the common things in both the decimal form?

46. The cost of a camera is reduced by 10% to make it equivalent to another camera having a selling price calculated on the basis of 10% profit on the cost price of 21,850. Find the original cost price of the first camera.

47. 3% of 600 is __________ less than 5% of 500.

48. A college offers 25% of all seats of the Graduate programme to local candidates. Last year 125 local candidates got admission in that college. Find the total seat capacity available in that college for Graduate programmes.

49. A shopkeeper offers two discounts of value 5% and 8% on an item. Calculate the equivalent discount of two such consecutive discounts.

50. Population of a city increases at the rate of 10% of previous year's population. Calculate the population of a city in which population before two years was 125,000. Also calculate the population of that city after two year.

51. Parking lot of a school is represented by an expression:

$$\frac{3}{4}\left(2(2 + 4k) + 2\left(3 + \frac{5}{6}k\right)\right)$$

Convert this expression in simplest form.

52. 30% of a number is equal to 40% of another number. Calculate the ratio of both the number.

53. $P = \sqrt{20} - \sqrt{20} + \sqrt{20} - \sqrt{20} \ldots \ldots \ldots \infty$. Find the value of $P^2 + 3P - 20$.

54. $\sqrt{15} = 3.88$. Find the value of $\sqrt{\dfrac{5}{3}}$.

55. A person moved on towards countryside at 6 O'Clock. He travelled certain distance at an average speed of 4 km/h, and then another distance at 3 km/h and again a distance at an average speed of 6 km/h. After reaching he turned back and reached the place from where he had started. That time it was 12 noon in his wrist watch. Find the distance travelled by him.

[Ans: 24 km]

56. A 500 m long train crosses a telephone post in 20 seconds. The same train crosses a platform in 90 seconds. Find the length of that platform.

[Ans: 1 km 750 m]

57. Two trains of length 200 m and 400 m respectively. They cross each other in 15 seconds while moving in opposite direction and 75 seconds while moving in the same direction. Find speed of both the train.

[Ans: 24 m/sec. and 16m/sec]

58. Normally Nikita performs her morning walk at an average speed of 12 km/h. Today her speed was $5/6^{th}$ of the average. Because of this reason she was late by 10 minutes. Find the normal time that she spends daily for morning walk.

[Ans: 50 minutes]

59. Speed of a train was reduced from 65 km/h to 50 km/h. Earlier this train was taking 1.5 hours to cover certain distance. Now it will take _________ minutes more to cover the same distance.

[Ans : 27]

60. In a kilometre race A beats B by 100 metres, B beats C by 100 metres. A beats C by _____ metres.

[Ans : 190 metres]

61. A bus moves a distance without stoppage at an average speed of 420 km/h. With stoppages the same distance is covered by that bus at an average speed of 28 km/h. find the hourly stoppage time of that bus.

[Ans: 20 minutes]

62. A 300 m long car is running at an average speed of 90 km/h. another car of length 200 m is running in the same direction at an average speed of 60 km/h. Find the time taken by the first car to overtake the second one.

[Ans: 50 seconds]

63. Length of a train is half that of a km long bridge. A train clears this bridge in 2 minutes. Find the speed of that train.

[Ans: 45 km/h]

64. A train of length 110 m passes a man, who is walking against it at an average speed of 6 km/h, in 6 seconds. The speed of this train is ____________.

[Ans: 60 km/h]

65. A boat running upstream takes hours 48 minutes to cover certain distance. It takes 4 hours to cover the same distance running downstream. Find the ratio between the speed of the boat and speed of the stream.

[Ans: 8:3]

66. What fraction of numbers in between 1 and 50 are prime numbers?

67. What least number must be added to 1029.1016 to make it exactly divisible by 1029?

68. Third multiple of a prime number which is greater than 90 and less than 100 = ______.

69. Complete the following:

a. $a^3 b^4 c^5 \times a^3 b^7 = $ _____

b. $a^5 b^8 c^5 \div a^3 b^7 = $ _____

c. $\dfrac{1}{\dfrac{1-\dfrac{1}{1-x}}{x-1}} + \dfrac{1}{\dfrac{1-\dfrac{1}{x^2-1}}{x+1}} = $ ________.

d. $\left(1 - \dfrac{9}{10}\right)\left(1 - \dfrac{99}{100}\right)\left(1 - \dfrac{999}{1000}\right) = 10 - - - - -$

70. Find the value of $\dfrac{m^2+1}{m^2-1} - \dfrac{m^2-1}{m^2+1}$,

if $\sqrt[3]{m} = \left(1 - \dfrac{1}{2}\right)\left(1 - \dfrac{1}{3}\right) \dots \left(1 - \dfrac{1}{1000}\right)$

71. If $\dfrac{2}{1 + \dfrac{1}{1 + \dfrac{x}{1-x}}} = 1$, then find the value

of $\left(\dfrac{x+1}{x-1}\right)^2 + \left(\dfrac{x-1}{x+1}\right)^2$.

72. Reciprocal of $x^8 = $ ____________.

73. A boat covers 30 km in 3 hours in the direction of a stream. It covers the same distance in opposite direction of the stream. Find speed of the boat in still water.

[Ans: 8 km/h]

74. Find the least number located in between 454003 and 354302 which is a multiple of 209. Also find other two factors.

75. What per cent is the least rational number of the greatest rational number, if $\dfrac{11}{12}, \dfrac{2}{3}, \dfrac{3}{4}, \dfrac{5}{9}$ and $\dfrac{17}{18}$ are arranged in ascending order ?

76. If $\dfrac{1}{891} = 0.00112233445566778899\dots$

Then what is the value of $\dfrac{198}{891}$?

77. If $\dfrac{p}{q} = 2.525252525 \dots \dots$

then find the value of $\dfrac{p^2+q^2}{pq}$.

78. A flower garden is 22.50 m long. Sheela wants to make a border along one side using bricks that are 0.25 m long. How many bricks will be needed?

79. The time taken by Rohan in five different races to run a distance of 500 m was 3.20 minutes, 3.37 minutes, 3.29 minutes, 3.17 minutes and 3.32 minutes. Find the average time taken by him in the races.

80. Anuradha can do a piece of work in 6 hours. What part of the work can she do in 1 hour, in 5 hours, in 6 hours?

81. Ravi can do half of a work alone in 12 days, Munish can do quarter of the same work in 18 days and Roushan can complete one tenth of the work in 2 days. If they all join hands to complete the same work then by what time the entire work will be finished?

82. What is the ratio of two numbers whose difference is 45, and the quotient of the greater number by the lesser number is 4 ?

83. Raj travels 360 km on three fifths of his petrol tank. How far would he travel at the same rate with a full tank of petrol?

84. It takes 17 full specific type of trees to make one tonne of paper. If there are 221 such trees in a forest, then what fraction of forest will be used to make; (a) 5 tonnes of paper. (b) 10 tonnes of paper? To save $7/13^{th}$ part of the forest how much of paper we have to save?

85. Find the value of $\dfrac{p+1}{p-1} - \dfrac{p-1}{p+1}$,

if $p = \left(1 - \dfrac{1}{2}\right)\left(1 - \dfrac{1}{3}\right)\cdots\left(1 - \dfrac{1}{100}\right)$

86. Fractions obtained on multiplying or dividing both numerator and denominator of a given fraction by the same non-zero number, and the given fraction are called ______________ fractions.

87. Find the value of

$$\left(1 + \frac{1}{2}\right)\left(1 + \frac{1}{3}\right) \cdots \cdots \left(1 + \frac{1}{1560}\right)$$

88. Find the value of p, if $p = \dfrac{0.2 \text{X} 0.14 + 0.5 \text{X} 0.91}{0.1 \text{X} 0.2}$

89. If $\dfrac{2}{1 + \frac{1}{1 + \frac{x}{1-x}}} = 1$, then find the value of $\dfrac{x+1}{x-1}$?

90. If x % of 16 = y % of 24, then find the value of $\dfrac{(x^2 - y^2)}{xy}$

91. If 1.5x = 0.04y then what is the value of $\dfrac{(y - x)}{(y + x)}$?

92. Find the value of p,

if $p = \dfrac{(6.4)^2 - (5.4)^2}{8.9^2 + 8.9 \text{ X } 2.2 + 1.1^2}$

93. Arrange in ascending order:

$$\sqrt{1.44}, \qquad 8^{\frac{1}{3}}, \qquad \sqrt[3]{0.027},$$

$$0.07 + \sqrt[2]{0.16} , \qquad \sqrt{3^2 + 4^2}$$

94. 13 hundredths is _____ % of 2.6.

95. $\dfrac{17}{15} X \dfrac{17}{15} + \dfrac{2}{15} X \dfrac{2}{15} - \dfrac{17}{15} X \dfrac{4}{15} = $ __________ .

96. Find the value of $p^2 + p + 1$, if $p = \dfrac{\left(\left(3\frac{1}{4}\right)^4 - \left(4\frac{1}{3}\right)^4\right)}{\left(3\frac{1}{4}\right)^2 - \left(4\frac{1}{3}\right)^2}$

97. 23% of a number is equal to the thousandth multiple of 92. Find three fifth of that number.

98. All the multiples of 9 are also multiples of _______, but all the multiples of _____ are not necessarily a multiple of 9.

99. Sum total of digits of ones and hundreds place is equal to the digit located at tens place. Number formed by last two digits is a greatest possible multiple of 4. Find the reciprocal of that number.

100. Municipal Corporation of a city has decided to organize plantation works beside a 25 km long road by placing trees beside both the sides of the road at an interval of 50 m. find the total number of trees that can be planted. Also find the cost of maintaining those plants at a rate of $ 2 for every 5 plants.

101. Half of a quarter of 98 = ______ .

102. Three bells toll at an interval of 12 seconds, 36 seconds and 45 seconds. After what time interval do they toll together? How many times do they toll together in a gap of three hours?

103. A train moving with a uniform speed of 72 km/h took 2.5 minutes to cross a light post. Find the time taken by it to cross a 1.8 km long platform.

104. Find the value of $\sqrt{272^2 - 128^2}$

105. The square root of 0.4444.... is ___________.

106. 4320 X p is a perfect cube value. Find the value of $p^2 + 3p + 9$

107. $\sqrt[3]{4\frac{12}{125}} = x$. Find the value of $3x^2 + 4x + 5$

108. $x^3 - 2mx\,2 + 16$ is divisible by $x + 2$. Find the value of m.

109. $2x^4 - px^3 + 3x^2 + 3x - 2$ is exactly divisible by $x^2 - 3x + 2$. Find the value of $p^2 + 3p + 17$.

110. Find the following:

$$64^a = \frac{1}{256^b},$$
$$i)\ 3a + 4b = \underline{\hspace{2cm}}$$

$$ii)\ \frac{(a+b)}{ab} = \underline{\hspace{2cm}}$$

111. Complete the following:

$$6^x - 6^{x-3} = 7740\ ;\ x^x$$

112. Find the value of $p^2 + 8p + 21$

$$p = \left(2^{\frac{1}{4}} - 1 \right)\left(2^{\frac{3}{4}} + 2^{\frac{1}{2}} + 2^{\frac{1}{4}} + 1 \right) = \underline{\hspace{2cm}}$$

113. Find the value of p.

$$a = (\sqrt{3} + \sqrt{2})^{-3}, \quad b$$
$$= (\sqrt{3} - \sqrt{2})^{-3},$$
$$p = [(a + 1)^{-1} + (b + 1)^{-1}]$$

114. Half a dozen banana costs $ 12. Find the cost of 20 bananas.

115. Arrange in ascending order.

$$16^{\frac{1}{2}}, \sqrt[4]{16}, \sqrt[2]{81}, \sqrt[3]{125}$$

116. Some bananas are to be shared among a number of children. To give each child 9 bananas would require 15 more bananas. But if the share of each is 8 there are 10 bananas left over. How many bananas are there?

117. In a number of three digits the unit's digit is double the tens' digit. The sum of the number and the number formed by reversing the digits is 1191 and the average of three digits is 5. What is the number ?

118. Is there any pair of number having HCF 121 and LCM 12321?

119. What least number should be added to five digit smallest number to make the number exactly divisible by 3, 6, 9, 18 and 27 without leaving any remainder in any case?

120. One fourth of one nineteenth of 76,076 = ...

121. Observe the following figure:

Statements

a. Both the figure represents fractions having same numerator.

b. If converted into like fractions, their denominators will be a common multiple of 20.

c. If we represent other three equivalent fractions of the sum total as $\dfrac{P}{60} = \dfrac{Q}{300} = \dfrac{R}{460}$, then P, Q and R will be multiples of 27.

d. Common denominator for both the fraction is also called a Greatest Common Divisor.

Which of the above statements are not correct?

Write your options: ______ ,

122. Find the smallest possible number of six digits divisible exactly by 12, 24, 36 and 72.

123. What is the smallest possible number of six digits divisible exactly by 11?

124. Complete the following:

1, 4, 9, __a____, __b____, ___c___;

Options	a	b	c
A:	16	25	36
B:	21	27	29
C:	12	15	19

Key Terms and Definitions

- acute angle (noun): any angle measuring between 0° and 90° – The leaves protrude out of the stem at an acute angle.

- add (verb): to combine two numbers to get a total – If we add 2 to 4, we get 6.

- addition (noun): the bringing together of two or more numbers to find a total – The addition of 2 new students to the class of 20 brought the total number of students to 22.

- ALGEBRA (noun): a branch of mathematics in which letters and other symbols can be used to represent numbers – It wasn't until I studied algebra that I got the concept of $E = mc2$.

- algorithm (noun): a set of rules used to carry out any calculation – Following this algorithm will make the problem easier to solve.

- angle (noun): the space (measured in degrees) between two lines which meet at a certain point – A square has four angles, whereas a triangle has three.

- arc (noun): a curved shape, the distance between any two points on the of the circumference of a circle – The sun moved in an arc across the cloudless sky from sunrise to sunset.

- area (noun): the two-dimensional space occupied by an object or shape – Malta is a small country with a surface area of 316 km2.

- ARITHMETIC (noun): the oldest and most basic branch of maths, dealing with numbers and their basic operations: addition, subtraction, multiplication, and division – There were 10 students in one class and 15 in the other, which if my arithmetic serves me right comes to 25 in total.

- ascending order (noun): increasing; arranged from smallest to largest – They told us to line up in ascending order of height, with the shortest on the left.

- average (noun): a mean; a number that is a typical representation of a set of numbers – To calculate the average of four different numbers for example, simply add the four numbers, then divide the total by four. So the average of 2, 4, 6 and 8 is 20 divided by 4 which is 5.

- axis (noun): an imaginary straight line around which a body rotates – The earth rotates on its axis which runs from North Pole to South Pole.

- base (noun): in geometry a base is the bottom line of a 2D shape such as a square or triangle, or the bottom surface of a 3D shape such as a pyramid – The statue stood on a heavy stone base.

- binary (adjective): relating to a system of numbers based on 2. See decimal – Computers use a "base-2" binary system of numbers 0 and 1.

- CALCULUS (noun): a branch of mathematics that studies continuous rates of change – Astronomers use calculus to track the orbits of different planets.

- capacity: (noun): the maximum volume that a container can hold – The tank has a capacity of 64 litres.

- cardinal number (noun): a number that expresses quantity (one, two, three etc), as opposed to an ordinal number which expresses position (first, second, third) – We started the lesson by learning about cardinal numbers.

- circle (noun): see shapes
- circumference (noun): The boundary of a circle or other curved geometric figure – The circumference of the wedding cake was 140 centimetres.

- common fraction (noun): a fraction expressed as a numerator above and denominator below, for example ½ (as opposed to decimal 0.5). Also called vulgar fraction – In practice, common fractions are often simply called fractions.

- cone (noun): see shapes

- consecutive numbers (noun): whole numbers that follow each other in ascending order without gaps – We can say that 7, 8, 9, 10, 11, 12 are consecutive numbers but 7, 9, 12 or 12, 8, 11 are not.

- coordinates (noun): usually a pair of numbers indicating a point on a graph (or map etc) – We read the first coordinate along the graph (left to right) and the second coordinate up the graph (bottom to top).

- cube (verb): when you cube a number you multiply it by itself three times – If you cube 3 you get 33 = 3 x 3 x 3 = 27. Three cubed is twenty-seven.

- cube (noun): see shapes

- cube root (noun): the cube root of a number is the factor that we multiply by itself three times to get that number. – 3 × 3 × 3 = 27 so the cube root of 27 is 3. The cube root of 8 is 2 because 2 x 2 x 2 = 8.

- curve (noun): a line that flows smoothly without any sharp turns – In maths a curve can be a straight line.

- cylinder (noun): see shapes

- decimal (adjective): relating to a system of numbers based on 10. This "base-10" system of numbers using 0-9 is derived from the Hindu-Arabic number system – Computers don't work with decimal numbers: they have to convert them into binary first.

- decimal point (noun): A full point or dot placed after the figure representing units in a decimal fraction – In English the decimal point is like a period (12.5) but in some languages, French for example, the decimal symbol is a comma (12,5).

- degree (noun): a unit of measurement for angles. The symbol is °. There are 90° in a right angle (an interior corner of a square) – Any angle less than 90° is called an acute angle.

- denominator (noun): The number below the line in a vulgar fraction – The teacher pointed to the denominator at the bottom of each fraction on the board.

- descending order (noun): decreasing; arranged from largest to smallest – Our exam scores were listed in descending order with the best at the top.

- diagonal (noun): a line that connects any two corners, but is not an edge – If you have a square and you join the top left corner to the bottom right corner, you get a diagonal.

- diameter (noun): The measurement of the longest distance across a circle, from one point to another – The table is over a metre in diameter and can easily seat four people.

- digit (noun): any of the ten Arabic numerals from 0 to 9 – The number 9 has only one digit, whereas 11 and 12 both have two digits.

- divide (verb): to break up a number into equal parts. We use the symbol ÷ (or the symbol /) to mean divide – We write $12 \div 3 = 4$ and we say twelve divided by three equals four. We can also write $12 / 3 = 4$.

- division (noun): The process of breaking up a number into equal parts. It is the opposite of multiplication. Division is represented by the ÷ symbol – The division of the class into four groups of 3 meant that we all got a chance to speak.

- edge (noun): a line between corners in 2D and 3D shapes – A square has four edges and a cube has 12 edges.

- equal sign (noun): the symbol = indicating that two amounts are of the same value, for example $2 + 2 = 4$ – I wrote down the answer on the right side of the equal sign.

- equation (noun): A mathematical statement which uses an equal sign (=) to indicate that two mathematical expressions are of the same value — The most famous equation ever is probably Einstein's $E = mc^2$.

- equilateral (adjective): having all sides the same length — By definition all squares are equilateral, but other shapes can be equilateral too.

- even number (noun): any integer (never a fraction) that can be divided exactly by two — The houses on the right side of the road all have even numbers | 2 and 4 are even numbers, whereas 1 and 3 are odd numbers.

- factor (noun): a number which produces another number when it is multiplied — Both 2 and 3 are factors of 6.

- formula (noun): a mathematical rule that can be written with numbers, letters and symbols — The formula V = l x w x h will give the volume of a box where V = volume, l = length, w = width and h = height.

- fraction (noun): a numerical representation of equal parts of a whole. If you cut a whole orange into two equal pieces, each piece is a fraction of the whole and can be expressed as 0.5 (decimal), ½ (common fraction), or 50% (percentage) — After the hungry children had finished their lunch, only a fraction of the pie remained.

- geometric, geometrical (adjective): relating to geometry — Much ancient Greek pottery was characterized by geometric patterns.

- geometry (noun): the branch of mathematics dealing with points, lines, surfaces, solids etc – I have a geometry test tomorrow.

- graph (noun): A diagram expressing the relationship of a set of numbers or measurements, usually with lines – The seasonal temperatures were shown on a graph with a single line going up and down.

- greater than: the symbol > means greater than or bigger than. See also < less than – If we write 5 > 3 we are saying that five is greater than three.

- hemisphere (noun): half of a sphere or three-dimensional round object – The earth's northern hemisphere and southern hemisphere are separated by the equator.

- infinity (noun): in maths, an imaginary number that is greater than any countable number; the symbol for infinity is ∞ – The infinity symbol is a closed figure of eight loop on its side indicating its unending nature.

- integer (noun): A whole number with no fractional parts – 3 is an integer, whereas 3.5 is not.

- less than: the symbol < means less than or smaller than. See also > greater than – If we write 3 < 5 we are saying that three is less than five.

- mean (noun): see average

- minus (preposition): with the subtraction of – Does 25 minus 10 equal 15?

- minus sign (noun): the symbol (-) indicating subtraction or a negative value – An example of the minus sign for subtraction is 5 - 3 = 2. An example of the minus sign for a negative value is that -10°C is ten degrees below freezing.

- multiplication (noun): the process of taking a number and adding it together multiple times. Multiplication is represented in expressions by the times symbol (x) – An example of multiplication is four times three (4 x 3) which is the same as 4 + 4 + 4 = 12.

- multiply (verb): to apply multiplication; to take a number and add it together multiple times – If you multiply 3 by 4, you get 12.

- negative number (noun): a number that is less than zero, typically preceded by a minus sign (-) or sometimes written in red – In 2 - 5 = -3, the result is a negative number.

- numerator (noun): the number above the line in a common or vulgar fraction – In ⅔ the numerator is 2 and the denominator is 3.

- obtuse angle (noun): an angle that is greater than 90° but less than 180° – The door was wide open at an obtuse angle.

- odd number (noun): any whole number that cannot be divided exactly by two. See even number – The number 23 is an odd number because it cannot be divided by 2.

- ordinal number↗ (noun): a number indicating the position of something within a list. Ordinal numbers show the "order" of things. They can be written in full (first, second, third etc.) or abbreviated (1st, 2nd, 3rd) – Unfortunately my horse came in third so I lost my money. | She was born on the 2nd of May.

- oval (noun): see shapes

- parallel (adjective): (of two lines) placed side by side with an equal distance between them at all points – The two planks of wood ran parallel to each other on the floor. Parallel lines never meet.

- percent (adverb): parts per hundred. The symbol is % – We sleep for about 30% of our lives.

- perimeter (noun): the total distance around a two-dimensional shape. The perimeter can usually be calculated by adding the length of all the edges together – Each edge of this square is 10cm, so the perimeter is 40cm.

- plus sign (noun): the symbol (+) placed between two numbers to indicate that the second number is being added to the first – An example of the plus sign for addition is 5 + 3 = 8, spoken as five plus three equals eight.

- pi (noun): the ratio of a circle's circumference to its diameter (circumference divided by diameter). Pi is approximately 3.14159 and is represented by the Greek symbol π – I calculated the circle's circumference by multiplying its diameter by pi. The value of pi is always the same regardless of a circle's size.

- polygon (noun): see shapes

- prime number (noun): a whole number greater than 1 that cannot be exactly divided by any whole number except itself and 1 – Four can be divided by 2, so it is not a prime number.

Seven can only be exactly divided by 1 and 7, so it is a prime number.

- PROBABILITY (noun): a branch of mathematics that predicts how likely something is to happen – When we toss a coin, the probability of it landing heads up is 50%.

- radius (noun): a straight line representing the distance from the centre of a circle to its circumference – The radius of the circle is half the length of the diameter.

- ratio (noun): a comparison of the quantity of one thing with the quantity of another thing – In our school there are 3000 students and 100 teachers, so the ratio of students to teachers is 30 to 1 (also written as 30 : 1).

- rectangle (noun): see shapes

- remainder (noun): an amount left over after division when the first number cannot be divided exactly by the other – 4 goes into 10 two times with the remainder of 2.

- right angle (noun): an angle measuring exactly 90°, such as an interior corner of a square. – If you draw a triangle with sides that are 3, 4 and 5 units in length, then you can create a perfect right angle using just a ruler.

- round up/down (verb): if you round a number, you make it simpler to use but keep it close to its original value - For example, you might round 43 down to 40. And you might round 47 up to 50.

- Shapes

- shape (noun): a geometric figure which can be 2D or two-dimensional (square, circle, triangle etc) or 3D or three-dimensional (cube, sphere, pyramid etc) – Geometry involves the study of all kinds of shapes, both 2D and 3D.

- 2D or two-dimensional shapes (flat)
- circle (noun): a round flat shape whose boundary is equidistant from its centre at all points

- oval (noun): any round flat shape that looks like an egg or "stretched circle"

- triangle (noun): a flat shape with 3 sides

- square (noun): a flat shape with 4 equal sides and 4 equal angles of 90°

- rectangle (noun): a flat shape with 4 sides and 4 equal angles of 90°. Opposite sides are parallel and of equal length

- trapezium (noun): any flat shape with 4 sides, none them parallel

- quadrilateral (noun): any flat shape with 4 sides

- pentagon (noun): a flat shape with 5 equal sides

- hexagon (noun): – a flat shape with 6 equal sides

- heptagon (noun): a flat shape with 7 equal sides

- octagon (noun): a flat shape with 8 equal sides

- polygon (noun): any flat shape with 3 or more equal sides

- 3D or three-dimensional shapes (solid or hollow)
- sphere (noun): a round 3D shape like a ball or globe. Every point on its surface is equidistant from its centre

- cone (noun): a 3D shape that tapers to a point from a flat circular base

- cube (noun): a symmetrical 3D shape with 6 equal square faces

- cuboid (noun): a 3D shape with 6 rectangular faces

- cylinder (noun): a 3D shape with straight parallel sides and a circular cross-section

- octahedron (noun): a 3D shape consisting of eight equal faces, twelve edges, and six corners

- prism (noun): a 3D flat-sided object with two identical ends

- tetrahedron (noun): a 3D shape with four triangular faces

- sphere (noun): see shapes

- square (noun): see shapes

- square root (noun): a number's square root (symbol $\sqrt{\ }$) is a smaller number whose product is the original number when multiplied by itself – The square root of 9 is 3 ($\sqrt{9} = 3$).

- subtract (verb): to take one amount or quantity away from another – If you subtract 3 from 10, you get 7.

- subtraction (noun): the process of subtracting one number from another. We use the minus sign (-) to indicate subtraction in maths – We practised our subtraction by removing pennies from the pile on the table.

- sum (noun): the amount which results from the addition of two or more numbers – 7 is the sum of 1, 2 and 4.

- three-dimensional, 3D (adjective): having 3 dimensions: length, breadth, depth. See 2D – Objects like boxes and buildings are 3D.

- times sign (noun): the symbol (x) that indicates multiplication – In multiplication we write 2 x 3 = 6 and say two times three equals six (or two multiplied by three equals six).

- triangle (noun): see shapes

- TRIGONOMETRY (noun): the branch of mathematics that studies triangles, their angles and lengths etc – Astronomers use trigonometry to figure out the distance of stars from earth.

- two-dimensional, 2D (adjective): having two dimensions: length, breadth. See 3D – Flat shapes like a triangle or a piece of paper are basically 2D.

- volume (noun): the amount of space occupied by any three-dimensional object, or that a three-dimensional object can contain; capacity – Three-dimensional objects have volume whereas two-dimensional objects have area.

- whole number (noun): integer; any number without fractional or decimal parts – 7 and 51 are whole numbers but 7½ and 51.3 are not.

Definitions:

- **Absolute value:** The distance a number is from 0.
- **Acute angle:** An angle that measures less than 90°.
- **Algebra:** The study of mathematical symbols and the rules for manipulating those symbols.
- **Algebra grid:** A grid used to illustrate values of algebraic expressions.
- **Angle:** The angle ∠ABC consists of the two rays from B that pass through A and C respectively. The spread between the directions of these rays is measured in degrees (°), and this measure is occasionally written m∠ABC, or sometimes ∠ABC, or even ∠B. 360° is a complete revolution.
- **Angle-Angle:** A way to tell that two triangles are similar, by comparing two angles in each triangle. Two triangles △ABC and △A'B'C' are similar when the measures of ∠A and ∠A' are equal and the measures of ∠B and ∠B' are equal.
- **Angle-Side-Angle:** A way to tell that two triangles are congruent, by comparing two angles and the side between them in each triangle. Two triangles △ABC and △A'B'C' are congruent when the measures of ∠A and ∠A' are equal, the measures of ∠B and ∠B' are equal, and the lengths of AB and A'B' are equal.
- **Area:** The size of a region in the plane, measured in unit squares (squares with side length 1).
- **Association:** A relationship or pattern linking the values of two variables.
- **Associative law of addition:** For any three numbers a, b, and c, it is always true that (a+b)+c=a+(b+c).
- **Associative law of multiplication:** For any three numbers a, b, and c, it is always true that (a(b))(c)=a(b(c)).

- **Base:** A number that is raised to a power.
- **Best fit line:** When the points on a grid are not all on a straight line, but seem to have a somewhat linear pattern, you can find a line that is the "best fit" (closest) to the points.
- **Break even:** Have a profit of zero (that is, make exactly as much money as you spend).
- **Circumference:** The distance around an entire figure, such as a circle or a sphere. For a sphere, this means the distance around a circle on the sphere whose center is at the center of the sphere.
- **Cluster:** A group of points in a scatter plot that are near each other.
- **Coefficient:** A constant that a variable or expression is multiplied by.
- **Combining like terms:** Using the distributive law to add any two multiples of an expression such as x. For example, you can simplify 4x+5x into 9x.
- **Commutative law of addition:** For any two numbers a and b, a+b=b+a.
- **Commutative law of multiplication:** For two numbers a and b, a(b)=b(a).
- **Conditional relative frequency:** A joint frequency divided by the total of its row or column in a two-way frequency table.
- **Cone:** A solid figure formed by taking a flat circular disk and extending it up to a single point.
- **Congruence rule:** A rule that allows you to tell that two figures are congruent by looking at some of their measurements, such as the Side-Angle-Side (SAS), Angle-Side-Angle (ASA), and Side-Side-Side (SSS) rules for triangles.
- **Congruent:** The same shape and size. Two plane figures are congruent if one can be obtained from the other by a rigid motion (a sequence of translations, rotations, and reflections).
- **Constant:** A single fixed number (unlike a variable, whose value can vary).

- **Converse to the Pythagorean Theorem**: If a triangle has side lengths a, b and c, and a2+b2=c2, then the triangle is a right triangle and c is the length of the side opposite its right angle.
- **Coordinates:** A point on a 2-dimensional plane is described by a pair (x,y). The coordinate x is given by the labels below the grid, and the coordinate y is given by the labels to the left of the grid.
- **Coordinate plane:** A 2-dimensional flat surface used for plotting points, lines, curves, and regions. It contains an x and a y axis which intersect at the origin.
- **Coordinate grid:** A grid of lines on a coordinate plane that makes it easy to see (x,y) coordinates of locations in that plane.
- **Corresponding angles:** Two angles that are formed by a transversal and each of the two lines that the transversal intersects, if the angles are in the same position relative to those lines. Usually we only talk about corresponding angles if the two lines are parallel, and in that case corresponding angles will have equal measures. Conversely, if any transversal creates two corresponding angles that are equal in measure, then the two lines are parallel.
- **Cost:** In economics, how much money a company spends to produce a product.
- **Cube:** The cube of a number x is x3, which is the volume of a cube whose edges each have length x.
- **Cube root:** The cube root of a, written 3√a, is the number whose cube is a. That is, (3√a)3=a.
- **Cubing:** Cubing a number x means computing the cube of x, namely x3.
- **Cylinder:** A solid figure formed by taking a flat circular disk and extending it straight up.
- **Data:** A collection of related measurements.
- **Decimal:** A fractional quantity written with a decimal point (like 0.5).
- **Decreasing function:** A function whose output decreases when its input increases.

- **Denominator:** The bottom number or expression in a fraction.
- **Difference:** The distance between two quantities, or the answer to a subtraction problem.
- **Dilation:** A dilation by a positive number r about a point A is a transformation that moves each other point B along the ray from A that passes through B, and multiplies distances from A by r. A is called the center of the dilation.
- **Distance:** The distance between two points A and B is the length of the line segment AB.
- **Distributive law of multiplication over addition:** For any three numbers a, b, and c, a(b+c)=a(b)+a(c), and (b+c)(a)=b(a)+c(a).
- **Distributive law of multiplication over subtraction:** For any three numbers a, b, and c, a(b−c)=a(b)−a(c), and (b−c)(a)=b(a)−c(a).
- **Equation:** A mathematical sentence with an equals sign (like 3x+5=11).
- **Equivalent:** Two fractions are equivalent if they have the same numerical value. Two equations are equivalent if they have the same solution set.
- **Expanding an expression:** Using the distributive law to turn expressions which need parentheses (like 3(x+2)) into expressions which do not (like 3x+6).
- **Exponent:** In a power, the number of times the base is multiplied by itself.
- **Expression:** A combination of variables and numbers using arithmetic (like 6−x).
- **Exterior angles:** The angles at each vertex of a polygon that are formed by one side touching that vertex, and the line extending the other side touching that vertex, and that are outside the polygon.
- **Formula:** An expression that is used to compute a value.
- **Fraction:** A numerator divided by a denominator (like 1/2). Usually we require the numerator and denominator to both be integers.

- **Frequency:** In statistics, the number of times something occurs, or is observed.
- **Function:** A rule that assigns to each input exactly one output. The graph of a function is the collection of points with coordinates (x,y), where x is an input and y is its corresponding output.
- **Geometry:** The mathematics of shape, size, position, and measurement.
- **Graph:** An image formed by plotting the solutions to an equation, or some other collection of pairs of numbers, on a coordinate plane. To graph an expression containing the variable x, set y equal to that expression.
- **Horizontal:** Going from side to side, like the horizon.
- **Hypotenuse:** In a right triangle, the side opposite the right angle.
- **Increasing function:** A function whose output increases when its input increases.
- **Improper fraction:** A fraction in which the numerator is larger than the denominator (like 3/2).
- **Infinite:** More than any finite (real) number.
- **Integer:** A whole number or the negative of a whole number. For instance, 37 and 0 and −5 are integers, but 2.7 and − 3/2 are not.
- **Interior angles:** The angles at each vertex of a polygon that are formed by the two sides meeting at that vertex, and that are inside the polygon.
- **Irrational number:** A number that cannot be written as a fraction m , n where m and n are integers.
- **Isolate:** Make a variable appear alone on one side of an equation, and not occur in the other side of the equation.
- **Joint frequency:** The number of events that satisfy both of two specified criteria.
- **Joint relative frequency:** A joint frequency divided by the total number of events.

- **Kilogram:** A kilogram, or "kg", is a mass that weighs about 2.2 pounds in normal Earth gravity.
- **Laws of exponents:**
- a(c+d)=ac + ad
- (ab)/d=(a/d) X (b/d)   , and   (ac)d=acd
- . These are always true when c and d are positive integers. If a and b are nonzero, then they are true for any integers c and d, as is
- A(c–d) = ac – ad
- If a and b are positive, then all four laws are true for any c and d.
- **Legs:** In a right triangle, the two sides next to the right angle.
- **Line:** An infinite straight collection of points with no gaps, extending in both directions. If A and B are distinct (different) points, there is exactly one line AB that contains them both.
- **Line segment:** The line segment AB consists of the points A, B, and the points on the line AB that are between A and B. AB is the straight path connecting A and B.
- **Linear:** A straight line, or an equation or expression whose graph is a straight line. If m and b are constants, then mx+b is a linear expression, and a function f defined by f(x)=mx+b is a linear function.
- **Linear association:** Two variables in a scatter plot have a linear association if the points form a pattern which is close to a straight line.
- **Linear function:** A function whose graph is a straight line.
- **Linear model:** An estimate for a variable using a linear expression in another variable.
- **Meter:** A length of about 39.37 inches.
- **Negate:** Take the opposite of a number, by multiplying it by –1.
- **Negative association:** A negative association between two variables means that when one increases, the other one usually decreases.
- **Negative number:** A value less than zero (like –3).

- **Nonlinear association:** Two variables in a scatter plot have a nonlinear association if the points form a pattern which is not close to a straight line.
- **Non-negative number:** A value which is not negative (it is either positive or zero).
- **Numerator:** The top number or expression in a fraction.
- **Obtuse angle:** An angle that measures more than 90°.
- **Origin:** The point on a coordinate plane where the x-axis and y-axis intersect. It is represented by the coordinates (0,0).
- **Outlier:** A value that "lies outside" (is much smaller or larger than) most of the other values in a collection.
- **Parallel:** Two lines in a plane are parallel if they always have the same distance between them, so they never intersect. If two lines are parallel, they have the same slope.
- **Perfect square:** A whole number which is the square of another whole number.
- **Perpendicular:** Two lines are perpendicular if they create a 90-degree angle. If two lines are perpendicular and the slope of one of them is m, then the slope of the other line is $-1/m$.
- **π:** ("Pi", pronounced like "pie.") The area of a circle with radius 1. A circle with radius r has area $\pi r2$ and circumference $2\pi r$. π is approximately 3.1416.
- **Plane:** A two-dimensional infinite flat collection of points, with no gaps or end in any of its directions.
- **Point:** A location. A point in the coordinate plane has coordinates (x,y), where x is given by the labels below a coordinate grid, and y is given by the labels to the left of a coordinate grid.
- **Point-slope form:** If a line contains the point (x1,y1) and has slope m, then its equation can be written as y−y1=m(x−x1). An equation in the form y−y1=m(x−x1) is said to be in point-slope form.
- **Polygon:** A finite number of line segments in a plane, with each segment starting where the previous one ends, and the first

segment starting where the last one ends, with no other intersections between segments. The segments are called "edges" or "sides."

- **Positive association:** A positive association between two variables means that when one increases, the other one usually increases also.

- **Positive number:** A value greater than zero (like 3).

- **Power:** An expression of the form ad. a is called the base, d is called the exponent, and ad is called "the dth power of a". If d is a positive integer, ad means a multiplied by itself d times.

- **Product:** The answer to a multiplication problem.

- **Profit:** Revenue minus cost.

- **Proportional sides:** A way to tell that two triangles are similar, by comparing all three sides in each triangle. Two triangles △ ABC and △A'B'C' are similar when there is a single number r such that the length of A'B' is r times the length of AB, the length of A'C' is r times the length of AC, and the length of B'C' is r times the length of BC. Conversely, if two triangles △ ABC and △A'B'C' are similar, then there is a positive number r with these properties.

- **Pyramid:** A solid figure formed by taking a flat base which is a polygon, and extending it up to a single point.

- **The Pythagorean Theorem**: If a right triangle has side lengths a, b, and c, where c is the length of the side opposite the right angle, then a2+b2=c2.

- **Quadrant:** Each of the four sections of a coordinate plane made by the intersecting x- and y-axes. The four quadrants are labeled I, II, III, and IV, counterclockwise from the top right.

- **Quadrilateral:** A polygon with 4 sides.

- **Quotient:** The answer to a division problem.

- **Radius:** The distance from the center of a circle or sphere to any point on the circle or sphere.

- **Rate of change:** The speed at which a variable changes over a period of time. This is given by the change in the variable divided by the change in (amount of) time.
- **Rational number:** A number that can be written as a fraction m/n where m and n are integers.
- **Ray:** A point A, together with all points in a single direction from A.
- **Reflection:** Rigid motion across a fixed line AB in a plane, like a mirror image.
- **Relative frequency:** A frequency divided by the total number of events, often expressed as a percentage.
- **Revenue:** How much money a company receives in sales.
- **Right angle:** A 90° angle.
- **Right prism:** A solid figure formed by taking a flat base which is a polygon, and extending it straight up.
- **Right triangle:** A triangle that has a 90° angle.
- **Rigid motion:** A motion that preserves distances and angle measures, with no stretching, shrinking, or bending. A rigid motion in the plane is a sequence of one or more translations, rotations, and/or reflections.
- **Root-mean-square error:** A number that tells you how far away a line or curve is from a collection of points (a smaller number means the line is a better "fit" to the points).
- **Rotation:** Rigid motion around a fixed center A, with turning but no reflection.
- **Scatter plot:** Dots in the coordinate plane representing pairs of linked measurements, such as heights and weights for a group of people.
- **Scientific notation:** Writing a nonzero number as $a \cdot 10n$ where n is an integer and $1 \le |a| < 10$ (that is, a has exactly 1 digit before the decimal point, and that digit is nonzero).
- **Side-Angle-Side:** A way to tell that two triangles are congruent, by comparing two sides and the angle between them in each

triangle. Two triangles $\triangle ABC$ and $\triangle A'B'C'$ are congruent when the lengths of AB and A'B' are equal, the lengths of AC and A'C' are equal, and the measures of $\angle A$ and $\angle A'$ are equal.

- **Side-Side-Side:** A way to tell that two triangles are congruent, by comparing all three sides in each triangle. Two triangles $\triangle$ ABC and $\triangle A'B'C'$ are congruent when the lengths of AB and A'B' are equal, the lengths of AC and A'C' are equal, and the lengths of BC and B'C' are equal.

- **Similar:** Two geometric figures are similar if they have the same shape but possibly different sizes, with corresponding lengths differing by a single common scale factor. In other words, two figures are similar if one can be obtained from the other by a similarity transformation. Two triangles are similar if they have the same angles as each other.

- **Similarity rule:** A rule that allows you to tell that two figures are similar by looking at some of their measurements, such as the Angle-Angle (AA) and proportional sides rules for triangles.

- **Similarity transformation:** A rigid motion followed by a dilation. Any combination of rigid motions and dilations has the same effect as some single rigid motion followed by a single dilation, so the entire transformation is a similarity transformation.

- **Simplify:** To rewrite an expression in a way that means the same thing but is simpler (or shorter). You can simplify $3x-x+6$ into $2x+6$.

- **Slope:** A number that measures how steep a line is. It shows the amount of change in the height of the line as you go 1 unit to the right. The slope of the line $y=mx+b$ is m.

- **Slope-intercept form:** The form $y=mx+b$ for a linear equation, where m and b are constants. The numbers m and b give the slope and y-intercept of the line that is the graph of that equation.

- **Solution:** In an equation, a number that can be substituted for the variable to make that equation true. If the equation has more than one variable, a solution is a list of numbers that when substituted for the list of variables makes the equation true. For a system of more than one equation, a solution must make all of the equations true.

- **Solution set:** All solutions to an equation or system.
- **Solve:** Find the solutions to an equation or system.
- **Sphere:** The set of points in space that are a given distance from a given center.
- **Square:** The square of a number x is x^2, which is the area of a square whose sides each have length x.
- **Square root:** A square root of a is a number b whose square is a. That is, $b^2=a$. If b is a square root of a, then so is −b. If a≥0, "the" square root of a, written $\sqrt{a}$, is the square root of a that is positive or zero.
- **Squaring:** Squaring a number x means computing the square of x, namely x^2.
- **Standard form:** For a linear equation, the form $Ax+By=C$ where A, B, and C are constants.
- **Statistic:** A number used to describe or summarize data.
- **Statistics:** The study of data, and the methods used to describe or summarize data.
- **Substitution:** In an expression or equation, eliminating a variable by replacing it with another expression that it is equal to.
- **Sum:** The answer to an addition problem.
- **Supplementary angles:** Two angles whose total measure is 180°.
- **System:** For equations, two or more equations that are all required to be true.
- **Term:** Element in a sum or difference.
- **Translation:** Rigid motion by a constant distance in a single direction, with no rotation or reflection.
- **Transversal:** A line that intersects two other lines in different points.

- **Triangle:** A polygon with 3 sides.
- **Two-way frequency table:** For events that can be divided into categories two different ways, a table of joint frequencies, using rows of the table to group the events one way, and columns of the table to group the events the other way.
- **Unit:** A standard measurement, such as a meter or an hour.
- **Value:** A number that a variable or expression can equal.
- **Variable:** A letter (like x) that we can use to mean different numbers at different times.
- **Vertex:** An end of a side of a polygon, or the corner point of an angle.
- **Vertical:** Going up and down.
- **Vertical angles:** Opposite angles formed by the intersection of two lines.
- **Vertices:** The plural of "vertex."
- **Volume:** The size of a region in space, measured in unit cubes (cubes with edge length 1).
- **Whole number:** One of the numbers 0, 1, 2, 3, … .
- **x-axis:** The horizontal line running through the origin on a coordinate plane.
- **x-coordinate:** The horizontal value in a coordinate pair. It tells how far to the left or right the point is. The x-coordinate is always written first in the coordinate pair.
- **x-intercept:** A point where a curve meets the horizontal axis (the x-axis).
- **y-axis:** The vertical line running through the origin on a coordinate plane.
- **y-coordinate:** The vertical value in a coordinate pair. It tells how far up or down the point is. The y-coordinate is always written last in the coordinate pair.
- **y-intercept:** A point where a line or curve meets the vertical axis (the y-axis). The y-intercept of the line $y=mx+b$ is the point $(0,b)$.